Scripture in Context Series

▲

Moral Questions of the Bible

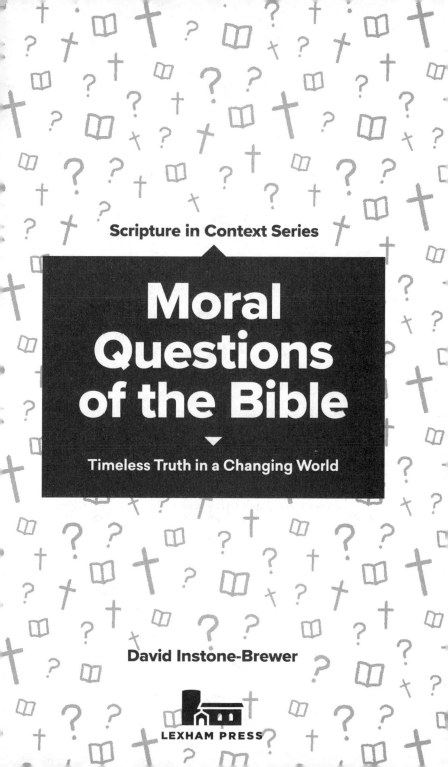

Scripture in Context Series

Moral Questions of the Bible

Timeless Truth in a Changing World

David Instone-Brewer

LEXHAM PRESS

Moral Questions of the Bible: Timeless Truth in a Changing World
Scripture in Context Series

Copyright 2019 David Instone-Brewer

Lexham Press, 1313 Commercial St., Bellingham, WA 98225
LexhamPress.com

Earlier versions of some chapters in this book appeared as articles in *Premier Christianity* magazine (www.premierchristianity.com). Used by permission.

Print ISBN 978-1-68-359295-2
Digital ISBN 978-1-68-359296-9

Lexham Editorial Team: Elliot Ritzema, Danielle Thevenaz
Cover Design: Owen Craft
Typesetting: Scribe Inc.

Contents

Section 2: Children

Section 3: Sex and Marriage

Section 4: Church Issues

Introduction

How do we use the Bible as a foundation for Christian morality? Answering this question is tough, because the world has changed a lot since Bible times, and even the New and Old Testaments are clearly different. So how can we decide which rules were for them and which ones still apply to us?

To take the Bible seriously requires hard work. We have to root around in the background to discover which issues the writers are addressing. In my own life, I've always been interested in the Bible, but I wandered down a very varied career path—social work, science technician, salesman, software engineer, etc.—before I gave in to a call to the ministry. After some years as a pastor, my denomination recommended me to the academic world to build on the work of my PhD in the Jewish background of the New Testament.

I now work at Tyndale House in Cambridge, UK, a biblical studies institute where scholars and pastors from every corner of the world meet, study, and exchange ideas and expertise. I am a senior research fellow, which means my job is to dig into whatever corners of the Bible and its ancient context interest me—a dream job in a dream setting!

Context is the key to understanding the Bible. Without it, we are reading the equivalent of ancient replies to lost letters, so we don't know what news or views they are responding to. We don't know whether the law of Moses is unusually strict or unexpectedly merciful if we don't know what was normal in the surrounding nations. We don't know whether Paul is telling people to fit in with Roman sensitivities or to take a stand against Roman vices if we don't know how Romans actually lived.

In my research I spend a lot of time in the company of ancient rabbis, who are known as Pharisees in the Gospels. Their determination to obey every nuance of the Old Testament law led them into some strange byways and debates as they strove to regulate daily life in order to guard against accidentally breaking God's law. The records of these debates give a fascinating insight into how Jews thought at the time of Jesus, and we can understand some of his teaching a lot better with this background knowledge.

I often quote these rabbis, and I've set up a website where you can read their legal discussions for yourself at www.RabbinicTraditions.com. Their earliest works, called the Mishnah and Tosefta, are the most important, because the early sections of these are the "traditions of [the] fathers" that Paul refers to (Gal 1:14). The Babylonian and Jerusalem Talmuds are later commentaries on them, though they often contain earlier material, and dating them is an academic interest of mine.

I also refer to other contemporary Jewish writers such as the sect at Qumran that wrote the Dead Sea Scrolls, preachers such as Philo, and historians such as Josephus, as well as Roman and ancient Near Eastern sources. These writings from the world of Bible times tell us about the lives of believers and their neighbors in the ancient world and about the moral dilemmas that they faced as they tried to honor God, follow Jesus, and witness to their neighbors. In a lot of ways they were rather like us, but the problems they faced were often different. Unless we understand them and the way they thought, we won't understand the Bible. It was written first for them—in their language, dealing with their problems—and second for all of us who lived later.

My working presupposition about the Bible is that it is God's personal message to humanity that has been remarkably preserved within the limits of scribal accuracy. I also presuppose that it was written by inspired humans and not by dictation from God. This means it is written in human language about human experiences, and it was understandable to the people of that time. Scholars are still debating exactly who wrote what, so as shorthand I will refer to authors such as Moses, Matthew, John, and Paul, since the message is just as powerful regardless of whoever was holding the pen.

The Bible is a translated book, so I always check the original Hebrew and Greek, though I only mention it when it matters. I'm on the NIV translation committee, so I know how difficult it is to bring out every nuance of the original in a single word or phrase.[1] Word-by-word translation is often misleading, especially when you have phrases like one found in Exodus 4:14, which could be translated as "The nose of the LORD grew hot against Moses." Translators know that in ancient Near Eastern culture this means that God was angry, so no Bibles mention God's nose in this verse! Sometimes, as our knowledge of culture deepens through archaeology and new texts, we discover new insights into the text. This can lead us to revise our interpretation as our understanding draws closer to that of the original writers, hearers, and readers. Although this is exciting,

---

1. I've helped create a website that enables anyone to follow the original text without knowing Greek or Hebrew—have a look at www.STEPBible.org.

I'm naturally cautious about new discoveries until they become well established.

In this book, I'm looking at lots of practical issues with an emphasis on how to find answers in the Bible. In the first section I set out the ways in which we can find answers for today's questions in a book that is thousands of years old. The other sections deal with examples—specific moral questions that we all face. My answers aren't final—you may come to a different conclusion when you know how to look for the information. But amazingly, I've found that the Bible has lots of insights into today's issues, because when you take the ancient context into account, it often throws light onto our own society.

Section 1

▾

Taking the Moral Questions of the Bible Seriously

1

▾

Can God's Law Change?

God doesn't change his mind, but he sometimes has to change his methods to achieve the same purpose. Laws that worked in the Old Testament world can have a detrimental effect today.

How can we find ethics for our world in the Bible, which was written for people living a few millennia ago? Our cultures are now so different that we can't simply use the same rules. Even in my lifetime, many cultural practices have changed. Men used to be expected to open the door for a woman, while expecting to get a higher salary than her for the same work. It used to be wrong to attend church in casual clothing. In the language of our grandparents, it was frowned on to "make love" in public (the old term for kissing), though everyone could have a "gay old time" like the Flintstones.

The Bible itself spans hundreds of years: Abraham and David lived about two thousand and one thousand years before Christ, respectively. It spans diverse cultures, too. Ancient Palestine was divided by rival warlords fighting for religious motives, with Israel in the middle. The Roman Empire dominated the Western world by imposing an overarching legal system enforced by overwhelming military power and was ruled by occasionally unstable figureheads. Looked at this way, not so much has changed, but ethically everything has changed.

Now we have solutions for malnutrition, most illnesses, and cold weather. Communication technology means that no one needs to be lonely. Safe abortions and reliable contraception have created a new freedom in human relationships. We can bomb people without setting foot in an enemy country or starve them by economic sanctions. All these advances simply prove that when circumstances become easier, we create new forms of human suffering. We need ethics now more than ever before.

It is a mistake to look for fixed rules in the Bible, because the Bible does not have fixed rules. Should we worship on a Sabbath or Sunday? The Sabbath was part of the Ten Commandments, but that didn't stop the early church from observing Sunday as "the Lord's Day." Should women cover their heads in church? Everyone agreed, from the emperor to a street cleaner, from the Jewish high priest to a drunk priest of Bacchus: all respectable women wore head coverings in public. But that changed too.

Can God change his mind? Balaam the pagan prophet said: "God is not human ... that he should change his mind," and Samuel, the first of the great Israelite prophets, agreed (Num 23:19; 1 Sam 15:29). And yet commandments, crimes, punishments, and dress codes changed through the Old Testament and into the New.

I don't think God changes his mind. His purposes are constant and unchanging, but in order to achieve them, he has to impose different rules, provide different incentives, and encourage different behaviors whenever different circumstances occur. If we want to find ethical guidance in the Bible, we can't fixate on the rules of one time or another. We need to discover the eternal purposes of God and consider how to achieve them.

IT'S NOT EASY CHANGING YOUR MIND

Changing your mind is hard, and almost impossible for some. Parents are afraid of being inconsistent, and politicians don't like being accused of doing a U-turn. This means that even when circumstances change or when new facts emerge, they have to find a way to claim "I've always said that." Religious leaders suffer in the same way—if they change their teaching, they can be charged with abandoning an ageless truth. If they honestly admit they were wrong, their following may abandon them for someone who claims to be never wrong.

The ancient world similarly regarded change as a sign of error or weakness. When Jews wanted to prove to their Roman neighbors that their religion was superior, they pointed out that the law of Moses was older than any Greek or Roman law or philosophy and that it never changes. No change is needed because God's law is perfect and timeless. But in practice, this wasn't true. What they never admitted was that they had changed the way the law worked, and some details in the Bible vindicate them for doing this.

The Bible contains many laws that we'd now regard as unethical. Persistent drunks should be stoned; people conquered in war should be wiped out; a poor Jew who can't repay a debt should be enslaved; and a childless widow should marry her brother-in-law—even if he already had a wife—in order to have a son (Deut 21:20–21; 25:5; 20:10–16; Lev 25:39–40). By the time of Jesus, these laws were mostly ignored in practice. The Jews knew that some laws had changed with time—for example, the law against shopping on the Sabbath wasn't introduced until the time of Nehemiah, at the same time that the once-a-lifetime Temple tax turned into the annual tax (Neh 10:31–32; compare Exod 30:11–16). So the law of God wasn't changeless.

The New Testament acknowledges that the law of God changes with circumstances—for example, when the priestly family changes, the laws about who can serve in the Temple have to change (Heb 7:12). This passage argues that the priesthood reached perfection and unchangeability in Jesus, but other circumstances still change.

When we read the Bible, we are looking over the shoulders of people living a few thousand years ago, for whom it was originally written. The law of Moses was revolutionary to them because it challenged them to live different lives. It didn't immediately transform them into a fully egalitarian society with a social-benefit system and legally protected human rights, but it did point them in that direction and pushed them as far as possible.

We can see what Israel would have been like without God's law by examining the laws of surrounding nations at the time. For example, if a man died without a son, these laws required his widow to produce an heir by sleeping with someone from her husband's family. This could be anyone—ranging from her husband's grandfather to his young nephew. But the law of Moses changed this in a humane way: it restricted this law to her husband's brother (i.e., someone roughly her age), and it gave her the choice to refuse.

U-TURNS WITHIN THE BIBLE

In the Old Testament, the death penalty applied to many crimes that we now regard as merely warranting imprisonment. However, imprisonment was impossible in a community that lived in tents and later in farm shacks. Even stone walls were easy to dig through before the invention of hard-setting mortar, so there was nowhere to lock people up securely.[1]

---

1. See chapter 21, "Is Gluttony a Sin?"

Even slavery becomes more acceptable when we realize it was often short term and voluntary. In exchange for wages in advance, someone would promise to work for up to six years in return for nothing but food and accommodation. Banks didn't exist, so this was a practical solution if your daughter needed a dowry quickly or your relatives were about to lose their farm. And Israelite slaves had more legal rights than employees in many countries today.[2]

Surrounding nations also had very different rules for warfare. Israel did kill or enslave people who attacked them, because letting them go merely resulted in another war a few years later, prompted by the honor-revenge culture of the time. However, surrounding nations carried out this draconian policy for *all* their enemies. By contrast, Israel was only allowed to kill conquered enemies who actually lived within their territory—that is, those who could sneak up for revenge during the night. When they conquered cities outside Israel, they should only kill those individuals who actually attacked them (Deut 20:10–17). Foreign leaders regarded Israel's rules of engagement in warfare as very generous (1 Kgs 20:30).

Israelite law regarded life as precious, especially in comparison to other nations. The law of Moses punished criminal injury with "an eye for an eye" all the way up to "life for life." However, the victim or her family could ask for financial compensation instead—and I guess that most people opted for this because it benefited them (Exod 21:23–30).[3] In surrounding nations,

---

2. See chapter 26, "Ending Slavery."

3. Financial compensation was specifically allowed for the most serious offense (v. 30), so it was assumed to apply to all others (*Mekilta de Rabbi Ishmael*, tractate *Nezikin* 8 [TinyURL.com/R-IshmaelExodus21-23]). Note that this book shortens internet links using TinyURL.com to make them easier to type into the address bar of your browser.

the punishment depended on whom you had injured. Physical punishment was compulsory if you injured one of the nobility, but if you injured an ordinary person the punishment was merely a fine, while the law of Moses had the same punishment whomever you'd injured, because everyone was equally precious. And in Israel, the penalty for theft was surprisingly mild—merely return the goods or their value plus a fine. However, in the surrounding nations, a thief was executed. In other words, Israel's law regarded all people as equal and regarded life as far more precious than things.

We can see that the law of Moses made sense back then, but is it still useful?

THE VALUE OF THE LAW TODAY

The Old Testament law's value today lies in its message about God's purposes, which are eternal. Through these laws, God taught Israel that people—all people—were supremely valuable. When you harvested your field, it was compulsory to leave something for the hungry poor. If you injured anyone, you were liable to severe punishment, even if that person was a slave or an unborn baby (Exod 21:20–23).

The Jews knew that God didn't change (Num 23:19; 1 Sam 15:29), but they also knew that the law had to change with circumstances if it was going to produce the same purposes that God intended. So when they returned from exile they felt free to change the details of the law in order to maintain those same purposes. Money and markets were much more common, and they needed to build a temple. So (as mentioned above) Nehemiah changed the once-a-lifetime Temple tax into an annual tax, and he banned markets on the Sabbath.

Increasing use of imprisonment meant that capital punishment was used much less often. By the time of Jesus, the Jews had found ways to avoid most executions; they expected God to carry out the death penalty for moral offenses by making someone die early. So when the Pharisees charged Jesus with drunkenness (using the wording of the capital offense in Deut 21:20; see also Matt 11:19), they didn't call for the death penalty. Of course, they did want to kill him, so they had to charge him with blasphemy, which was regarded as much more serious.

Jesus and the early Christians changed the laws of the Old Testament much more. Jesus ruled out polygamy, which the Old Testament allowed and even encouraged for a child-less widow (Deut 25:5–6).[4] Paul abrogated the law of the childless widow, saying that she could marry whomever she wanted (1 Cor 7:39).[5] Paul probably wanted to sweep away other laws too, because he regarded women, slaves, and non-slaves as completely equal. But instead, he advocated voluntarily keeping the status quo for the sake of the gospel (Gal 3:28).[6]

God's principles are unchangeable. He wants people to have a day of rest—Saturday or Sunday, or both; the exact rule doesn't matter. God wants everyone to be respected, so we should follow whatever dress codes demonstrate that. The modern equivalent of women neglecting to wear head coverings might be a see-through blouse. This would be OK in a nightclub, but not in church or in other formal settings. Dress codes change, but principles don't.

God's laws in the Bible constantly pushed humanity forward in order to change them for the better—in the areas of punishment, equality, and care of the oppressed. God's law changed people as much as they could be changed at the time. This means

---

4. Jesus restricted marriage to only two people (Matt 19:4; see also Gen 2:24).
5. See chapter 11, "Jesus Outlawed Polygamy."
6. See chapter 14, "Wifely Submission."

that some details of God's laws changed when society and circumstances changed. The unchangeable nature of God's law lies in the underlying principles and purposes: the most valuable things on earth are people, not commodities. This is the unchanging ethical principle of the Bible. God supremely loves and values people, and his law teaches every generation to do the same.

But how do we know when a law can change—such as the day of the week on which we rest, or one's dress code? And which laws are changeless—such as the law against murder or theft? How do we discern what can be changed from what is unchangeable? The next chapter finds clear guidelines.

2

▼

Finding Fixed Morals for a Changing World

New Testament Christians act differently from Old Testament saints, so how can we know what is right for modern-day Christians? We can work it out, case by case, from the historical and biblical context.

The main question of this book is, Can we use the Bible as a basis for morality? Society and technology change so fast that any set of rules quickly becomes outdated. So how can a book that was written to be relevant a few thousand years ago provide rules that still apply today?

If you are someone who likes reasons and overarching theories about how things work, read on. If your mind works better with examples from real life, you might prefer to skip this chapter. You can always come back to it when you want to consider general principles.

Saying that the Bible is inspired doesn't solve the problem. You may believe that the books of the Bible were written by clever people helping their own society to follow God. Or you may believe (as I do) that these writers were given supernatural help. In theory they could have been told what society would be like thousands of years later. But if they included rules for every society in every culture in every age, this would produce a very large and strange book. There would be too many ifs and buts!

Here's an example of a Bible rule that seems clear at first glance but may require deeper scrutiny: Paul's command for women to cover their heads in worship (1 Cor 11:5). An Australian told me about the surprise his friend had when he first preached in rural churches of Papua New Guinea, where they cope with the heat by wearing very minimal clothing. Some churches had a row of Western women's hats just inside the door, so he got used to seeing topless women wearing incongruously ornate hats during the service in obedience to Paul's command. Other churches didn't have these hats, so the women, similarly topless, took off their skirts and put them over their heads when entering the church. They believed that all of God's commands in the Bible are timeless, and there isn't any specific command in the Bible about covering anything except the head.

We clearly need some way to identify which commands in the Bible should be obeyed at all times and which ones need to be adapted in different cultures.

RULE OF LOVE

Some people think that we can throw away all the commands in the Bible except one: love. Of course Jesus, Paul, and Augustine all said that love is a good summary of the commandments, but this didn't stop Jesus from listing the Ten Commandments (Matt 19:18–19 = Mark 10:19 = Luke 18:20) or stop Paul from giving his congregations lots of specific teaching.

In the modern world, Joseph Fletcher's *Situation Ethics* argues this position well.[1] He says that in every situation whatever

---

1. Joseph Fletcher, *Situation Ethics: The New Morality* (Philadelphia: Westminster, 1966).

results in the greatest love (which he equates roughly with justice and benefit to people) is what we should do. There are no set rules or commands that we can glean from the Bible because every situation is different, and specific rules will always be changeable. This sounds great until you get to specific, complex moral issues, or a situation where following the normal rule would have unintended bad consequences for other people. And it tends to result in a moral code that "feels right" to the individual because, after all, what seems more loving than free love?

TRYING TO IDENTIFY
TIMELESS CATEGORIES

For those of us who regard God's revelation in the Bible as important, we need to find some way to distinguish commands that were made for a certain time or culture from those that are timeless—the ones that apply in every culture. We don't want to pick and choose the commands we'd like to obey; we want to know which ones we *should* obey and which ones don't apply to us now. So we need a rule by which we can decide which commands are timeless.

One common method is to divide Bible commands into different categories, such as:

1. Social rules for behavior, which warrant shame if broken

2. Religious observances, which warrant a sin offering (and perhaps punishment)

3. Criminal laws, which warrant punishment by the state

We wouldn't expect the social rules to be timeless because they depend on the norms of society. And we know that religious observances aren't timeless because the Old Testament rites were fulfilled by Jesus. However, we do expect criminal laws to be timeless because things such as murder are always wrong in any society.

So far, this looks like a good, objective method for identifying timeless commands. But this neat solution breaks down as soon as we attempt to put particular commands into those categories. Here are some examples that we'll be looking at later, from both the Old and New Testaments:

1. Social rules: honoring parents, deference to older people, women's head covering

2. Religious observances: Sabbath rest, sacrifices, no idolatry, Jews marry only Jews

3. Criminal laws: polygamy, adultery, rape, manslaughter, charging interest, slavery

We can immediately see some problems. We would expect the social rules to vary in different societies, but even this short list includes two that we'd expect to find in absolutely all societies: honoring parents and deference to older people. We would also expect religious observances to vary in different cultures, but these include commands that we'd expect everywhere, such as prohibiting idolatry. And we would expect criminal laws in the Bible to be timeless so that they would apply in every culture, but the Bible includes laws that regulate things we wouldn't want to promote in *any* culture, such as polygamy and slavery.

Perhaps we can solve this by refining our selection process. We could, for example, decide that the New Testament determines whether a command is timeless. In that case, we could assume that social and religious laws *become* timeless if they are reaffirmed in the New Testament, and that criminal laws are *only* regarded as timeless if they are reaffirmed in the New Testament.

In that case, our refined selection would leave us with:

1. Social rules: honoring parents, deference to older people, women's head covering

2. Religious observances: Sabbath rest, sacrifices, no idolatry

3. Criminal laws: adultery, slavery

This refinement to our selection process has solved a lot of our problems, though not all of them. We wanted to include honoring parents and deference to older people as rules for every society, and this succeeds in doing that, because they are affirmed in the New Testament (Matt 19:18 = Mark 10:19 = Luke 18:20; 1 Pet 5:5). However, this new selection also includes women's head coverings, so by this selection process we'd have to accept this as a timeless command because it is affirmed in the New Testament (1 Cor 11:5-6, 10, 13).

With regard to religious observances, the New Testament refers to worship on the Sabbath by Christians (Acts 13:14, 42; 16:13; 17:2; 18:4). Also (surprisingly), Temple sacrifices were still being used by at least some Christians in the New Testament. Christians such as Peter continued visiting the Temple, and Paul even made the sacrifices needed for ending a Nazirite vow, paying for these sacrifices for some other Jewish Christians (Acts 2:46; 3:1; 18:18; 21:26). Paul and others said it was wrong to *rely* on sacrifices for salvation, but there was clearly nothing wrong with using sacrifices as a way to worship God (Rom 3:20; Gal 3:10; 5:3-6; Heb 10:1-10). So, seeing that sacrifices are commanded in the Old Testament and carried out by New Testament

Christians, by this selection process we'd have to conclude that sacrifices are included in the timeless commands from God.

We have similar results with criminal laws. If we refine their selection by saying that they need to be reaffirmed in the New Testament, this removes some problems but not all of them. Polygamy isn't affirmed in the New Testament—indeed, Jesus abrogates it.[2] And the law against charging interest isn't mentioned in the New Testament, so we don't have to close all our bank accounts because we can conclude that this law isn't timeless. However, the New Testament doesn't mention the Old Testament laws against rape and doesn't distinguish between murder and manslaughter, which would imply that these laws aren't timeless either (Deut 4:42; 19:4–5; 22:25–27). Yet I can't imagine any society where these laws aren't needed.

No doubt we could continue to tinker with the selection criteria until we are finally left with a sensible list of timeless commands. But the more tinkering we do, the more it would become obvious that we are choosing which ones to keep and then fixing the criteria in order to select them. In other words, we are cheating, because we are doing the same as picking and choosing the ones we like best.

In this book I will attempt to use another method. This method also aims to be objective, but takes into account the cultural context for the commands.

BIBLE COMMANDS IN THEIR CONTEXT

This book will seek to find out which biblical commands are timeless by examining their effect in the culture of the time in which they were given. Having done that, it should be possible to work out how to achieve those same purposes today.

---

2. See chapter 11, "Jesus Outlawed Polygamy."

Discovering the purposes behind the commands is really important, because we can assume that God's purposes are eternal, though the means by which to carry out a given purpose in different societies may vary.

We can discover the purpose of a command by looking at the original culture. In particular, we see that some commands are countercultural—that is, God's people were expected to live differently from other people in that same culture. But other commands reflect the best of the current culture—that is, they identified and commended the *good* rules and norms of the society that these believers lived in. This difference is important, because we'd expect countercultural commands (such as rejecting idolatry) to be timeless, but culture-reflecting commands (such as women covering their heads) would not necessarily apply in another culture. This method is being increasingly used by those working with Bible ethics, partly because it takes the background of the Bible seriously and partly because it works.[3]

Some quick examples will help to illustrate this. The various chapters in this book explore many other examples in detail.

Countercultural commands. An example of a countercultural command is the one against idolatry. The Bible consistently forbids idolatry throughout both Testaments, and this contrasted with the prevailing cultures throughout Bible times. The societies surrounding Israel in the Old Testament and the Roman society in which New Testament Christians lived were full of idols and their worshipers. This is a command that we would expect to apply in any culture, whether other people agreed with it or not.

---

3. See Volker Rabens, "The Bible and Ethics: Pathways for Dialogue," *In die Skriflig* 51, no. 3 (2017) (TinyURL.com/BibleEthics).

In most Western societies it is easy to obey this command, because hardly anyone worships idols in the way that ancient people did. However, it can be very difficult in some rural African societies, because rejecting idolatry and the associated religions will cut you off from the witch doctors, and they may be your only source of herbs and medical advice in a rural situation.

In general, countercultural commands are timeless. If believers were called to make a stand against the culture they lived in by doing the opposite of what most other people were doing, then this is likely to be very important to God's purposes. Believers should regard this as God's message to them that they should stand up against those who do not obey this command.

Universal, culture-reflecting commands. The Bible has many commands that reflect the cultures of both Old Testament and New Testament times and also cultures in our own times. For example, all these cultures have rules against theft, murder, adultery, and so on.

Societies might define these things differently, of course. Some cultures do not consider it murder if you are avenging the murder of a family member, and some cultures expect the leader of a family to carry out a capital sentence on family members—the Roman society of New Testament times expected this. Similarly, some cultures do not regard it as stealing if you take something from a thief who has stolen from you, but this could land you in jail in most modern societies. Adultery is considered wrong in almost all cultures, but few today would regard it as a criminal offense.

Nevertheless, putting aside these differences in detail, we will find that if a command in the Bible agrees with that found in all societies, including our own, it is timeless. We should regard it as part of God's natural revelation to the whole of humanity, which we should always obey.

IDENTIFYING COMMANDS
THAT ARE NOT TIMELESS

The commands in the two groups above (countercultural commands and universal, culture-reflecting commands) are all likely to be timeless. Commands that are already universally followed by all societies will no doubt apply in all future societies. And we would expect countercultural commands to be timeless because if God asked his people to act completely differently from those living around them—a difference that might even endanger them—we'd expect this to be important enough to apply in every society.

The only possible exception would be if a countercultural stand achieved a purpose in that society that could be achieved in a different way in another society. For example, the Methodists and Salvation Army took a countercultural stand against alcohol when it was ruining society, with the purpose of helping prevent addiction, but many would argue that this stand no longer achieves that purpose. This stand against alcohol was not, of course, commanded in the Bible, but it shows that it is possible that a countercultural command may not be timeless. I can't think of an example in the Bible, but we should be aware that this is a theoretical possibility.

Commands that don't fit into either of the two categories above are the most interesting ones, because they are likely to not be timeless. To decide whether they are timeless, we have to carefully consider their purpose in the original culture and ask whether they still fulfill that same purpose in our culture.

Non-universal, culture-reflecting commands. A command may reflect one set of cultures, but not others. For example, dress codes vary dramatically even within the modern world. In many parts of the world it is indecent for a woman to show the skin of her legs or arms, but in other countries it is OK, and on most beaches she can show almost all of her skin.

It is clearly a good idea to follow the dress codes of the culture you live in. Western women who visit traditional Arab countries are expected to cover up, though not necessarily to the same extent as locals. If you are hoping to evangelize in those countries, you will certainly want to fit in with the culture as much as possible so that your message isn't rejected out of hand as a "foreign" religion. If this kind of culture-reflecting command did exist in the Bible, we'd certainly want to follow it in cultures that this command reflected.

But would a command that reflects some cultures in Bible times always apply in other cultures? In this case, if there were a culture-reflecting command in the Bible that a woman may not reveal any of her leg or foot, would all Christian women have to wear trousers and socks? This is a live and contentious issue because Paul told Corinthian believers that women should cover their heads (1 Cor 11). This reflected the Roman culture of the time, so it could be regarded as a non-universal, culture-reflecting rule. But it might also be one that should be applied universally—how could we decide?

Before looking at the method used to solve this, let's acknowledge another set of commands that cause problems: the changeable ones.

Changeable commands. Sometimes God appears to change his mind, as we saw in the previous chapter. In the Old Testament, believers could marry more than one wife or volunteer to be a slave. But in the New Testament Jesus argues against polygamy, and Paul says you shouldn't seek to be a slave (1 Cor 7:23).[4]

---

4. Some people did this in order to become a Roman citizen after being freed from slavery.

The biggest group of changeable commands are those concerning how to worship God and how to live in holiness. The Old Testament commands about sacrifices and purification rites such as immersion and sprinkling with blood are clearly not commanded in the New Testament. Christians were allowed to continue sacrificing in the Temple while it remained standing, but no sacrifices were commanded. Christians didn't have to bathe before worship, even if they had been in the same building as a corpse or if they had touched a menstruating woman. Even the food laws lapsed.

If we assume that God didn't actually change his mind, this means that these commandments didn't represent the actual purpose that God wanted to achieve. They were the means toward achieving another purpose.

For example, the worship of God changed from outward rites to inner spirituality. The reason was the Holy Spirit: as a result of Jesus' death, believers could be clean enough to have the Holy Spirit within them. So the emphasis shifted from outward purity to inner purity by moral lifestyles and by immediate confessing of any sins that did occur. These different sets of commands in the Old and New Testaments achieved the same purpose: believers could worship God in the closest and most personal way possible at the time.

Similarly, the changing laws of polygamy achieved a consistent purpose—they enabled the maximum number of people to find comfort and security in marriage. In the Old Testament there were too few men, especially during times of war, so without polygamy many women would have been left unsupported. By New Testament times, the numbers of men and women were roughly equal. This meant that rich men could have more than one wife, and many poor men were left on their own. Forbidding polygamy put that right. So the command had to change when the circumstances changed; otherwise, it wouldn't achieve God's changeless purpose.

HOW DO WE DECIDE THE COMMANDS FOR OUR CULTURE?

Timeless commands are therefore:

1. **Countercultural commands**, by which believers are told to stand out and live differently from the culture around them

2. **Universal, culture-reflecting commands**, by which believers are told to emulate the universal moral rules found in all cultures

Other commandments are not timeless, although the purposes of God that they attempt to promote *are* timeless:

1. **Non-universal, culture-reflecting commands**, by which believers are told to emulate some aspects of the culture they live in that aren't found universally in all cultures

2. **Changeable commands**, by which the Bible's teaching changes from one time or place to another

When commands aren't timeless, we can still look for the timeless purpose of God behind those commands. This is the method that is applied in later chapters of this book. All believers want to achieve the purposes of God, but this can't be done by blindly following whatever was commanded in the past in different circumstances and cultures. If that same purpose is still achieved by following the same command, then it still applies, but if the same purpose is achieved by a different route, we should consider that.

For non-universal, culture-reflecting commands, we have to look at each one on a case-by-case basis. This isn't straightforward, but it isn't too difficult either.

For example, if a command did exist in the Bible about covering women's legs, the context might indicate that this conformed with a common code of decency, so it would hinder evangelism if that rule were ignored. If this were the purpose, and God's purposes don't change, we'd have to consider whether that command still fulfilled the same purpose in our culture. It seems very unlikely that evangelism would be aided if all Christians dressed in strange clothing. So, in this hypothetical example, it seems unlikely that this command should be followed in all cultures.

For changeable commands, we can also assume that God has an unchanging purpose that can be achieved by different commands in different contexts. Here too, we have to identify the purpose that those commands were achieving in their original context and discover which command would achieve that same purpose within the context of our culture.

THE TWO TESTS FOR TIMELESSNESS
We now have two tests that we can apply to any command we find in the Bible. We can ask:

1. Is this command expressed or implied in the same way throughout the Bible?
In practice this usually means comparing the Old and New Testaments. Sometimes the absence of the equivalent command in one or the other will be incidental, but we have to be open to the

possibility that its absence indicates that it no longer applies. The absence of a law against rape in the New Testament is probably because no one needed to be told that this was wrong, but the absence of laws about leprosy implies they no longer apply.

If a command is found in both Testaments, it is most likely a timeless command, especially if the answer to the second question is also positive.

2. Is this command countercultural in at least one situation?

The command may be countercultural only for ancient Israel, or only for New Testament Christians, though usually it will be countercultural in both situations. That God's people are expected to follow this command *in spite of* the culture they are in implies that they would be expected to follow it in every other culture.

This process of asking two questions sounds simple, and often it is. But there can be disagreements about what the purpose of the command was in the original culture. Sometimes the Bible does not tell us enough about the culture—after all, why should it, seeing as it was originally written for people who were living in that culture and didn't need to be told? So we often have to do some work and research that culture.

So it is both easy and hard, exciting and frustrating—but it is worth doing if we want to fulfill the purposes of God.

3

▾

Focusing on the
Purposes behind the Laws

The psalmist loves God's commands, but they can become a burden when applied wrongly. Jesus criticized Pharisaic stringency, but the church soon started down similar paths.

Rules are useful and good, and the Old Testament law is praised in the Psalms as a sweet source of joy (Ps 119:103, 111). But rules can also be ugly and deadly when they are applied in a legalistic way. The term "Jobsworth" was popularized by Esther Rantzen's British TV show *That's Life!* (1973–1994). The show awarded a weekly "Jobsworth" peaked cap to the most annoying officious person who applied the rule book against all reason, saying, "It's more than my job's worth to break the rules." An example was the inspector at a members-only fishing area who fined a woman for holding her husband's rod while he attached a maggot to the hook, because only her husband had a license for using a rod.[1]

The commands of the Old Testament were at the heart of religious life for the Pharisees in Jesus' time. To be fair, they had

---

1. See BBC News, "Your Job's Worth More Than You Are" (TinyURL.com/JobsworthStory and TinyURL.com/JobsworthPhotos).

a good reason for loving these commands: they wanted to serve God, and seeing that God had given these commands, the least they could do was obey them. Unfortunately, this well-meaning principle led them to invent many new rules, which extended into absurd details. They called these rules a "fence" around the law, because their aim was to make sure that no one ever got *close* to breaking God's commandments. However, their new rules sometimes contradicted God's purposes that lay behind the commands themselves.

SEVEN WEEKS' VACATION

For example, God commanded a day off once a week, which makes fifty-two days a year—over seven weeks' holiday! But the Pharisees regarded it as a law, not a benefit, so they wanted to make sure that you didn't accidentally perform even minor work on that day by adding the rule that you shouldn't carry any tools on the Sabbath. This included anything as small as a needle pinned to your clothes, because you might be tempted to repair a hem on the Sabbath without remembering that this was "work." The definition of "work" gradually included more and more things. By the first century AD they had a list of thirty-nine categories of work. In Jesus' day they added the category of "healing," which included giving medicine or rubbing in ointment. By the end of the century even praying for healing was forbidden as work.

On the Sabbath you couldn't even rescue someone who'd fallen into a pit—unless they were likely to die before the end of the Sabbath (at least they recognized that saving a life overrides other commands). Even then, you had to pull them out with something like a coat—not with a rope, because this was a "tool." Falling into a pit was a regular occurrence because many properties had plaster-lined cisterns to store rainwater, which fell heavily but infrequently. Water cisterns had straight, smooth sides and were often very deep—the one found at the Masada fortress is as large as a four-story house! Joseph, David, and Jeremiah all knew what it was like to be stuck inside one that was full of mud (Gen 37:24; Ps 40:2; Jer 38:6), but if it was full of water, you wouldn't survive long. Jesus asked rhetorically: Which of you wouldn't help an animal out of a pit on a Sabbath? (Matt 12:11; Luke 14:5). The sad truth was that strict law-abiding Jews wouldn't even help a human.[2]

Jesus didn't treat the Sabbath as a set of rules; he regarded it as a gift from God. He said: "The Sabbath was made for man, not man for the Sabbath" (Mark 2:27). God's purpose was to give us a rest one day a week—for our own benefit. So God certainly wouldn't want us to come to harm by obeying this law too strictly.

DID JESUS AGREE WITH GOD'S LAW?

Jesus didn't reject the Old Testament law. He actually told his followers to observe it *more* strictly than the Pharisees (Matt 5:17–20). But instead of the *letter* of the law, Jesus identified the *purpose* of God behind the commands. And he said that God's purpose for the Sabbath law was to give people and servants a rest.

Jesus also identified the purpose behind other laws. For example, behind the law against murder Jesus identified God's purpose that we should avoid all hatred (Matt 5:21–26). Similarly, the law against adultery indicates God's purpose that we should avoid all inappropriate sexual fantasies; the law against wrongful divorce indicates God's purpose that marriage vows should

---

2. See, e.g., the rules at Qumran (Damascus Document 11:13–18 = 4Q270 [on p. 177 of TinyURL.com/VermesScrolls]).

never be broken; and the law "love your neighbor" was intended to include everyone, even enemies (Matt 5:27–48).

Jesus demonstrated the way in which we should read Old Testament commands. We need to ask what God's purpose was: Why did God give *that* command to people in *those* circumstances? The Old Testament commands were given to the simple, rural community of ancient Israel. They were surrounded by nations with no basic rights for slaves or animals and with detestable religious practices including child sacrifice. Israel therefore needed laws about religious purity, basic human rights, and farmyard hygiene. They also needed harsh penalties because they had no prisons where they could attempt rehabilitation.

Unfortunately, later rabbis continued to ignore what the original purposes of the laws were. They simply reapplied the ancient, rural law code instead of looking for God's purposes. They decided that flicking a light switch on a Sabbath was performing labor because the spark in the plug was equivalent to lighting a fire. And banning the ancient, barbaric practice of cooking a kid in its mother's milk was extended to mean that you can't cook any meat in a pan previously used for dairy products.

God's purposes for humanity don't change—whatever God wanted in the past is the same as what God wants for us now. Instead of applying the details of the old commands strictly, we need to find God's *purpose*, like Jesus did. We should find laws that have the same effect as the original ones. That way, the purpose that God wanted to achieve by those ancient laws would be achieved in the new situations.

Having identified these purposes of God, we must take care not to promote them to an inspired status, because we can get it wrong. Jesus criticized the Jews for "teaching the commands of men as if they were doctrines [of God]" (Matt 15:9; Mark 7:7, author's translation). We might be tempted to think that our understanding is so perfect that we can teach our interpretations as if they are God's words. Priests serving communion in Anglican churches have to wear "a white surplice with sleeves"[3] because this was decent dress in the seventeenth century—but such rules have the habit of fossilizing without regard to their purpose. They are based on our conclusions about what God was doing in that society, so we must always be open to a deeper understanding of God's intentions.

It would be so much easier if God could simply give us a new rule book periodically—one for each culture in the world—so that, like children, we could be told what to do in any circumstance. Jesus spoke of believers as children of God, and the New Testament letters continue using this imagery, but it has limits. Paul and the writer to the Hebrews complained about believers who refuse to grow out of their infancy—they still wanted baby's milk when they should be chewing on the meaty bits of Scripture (1 Cor 3:1–2; Heb 5:12–14). God expects us to use our brains as well as our bodies to serve him. However, the church has often fallen into the trap of inventing new rules on God's behalf to save us the bother of thinking for ourselves.

NEW PHARISEES IN THE CHURCH

The church actually has a worse record than the Pharisees for inventing new rules and enforcing them increasingly stringently. The ancient rabbis emphasized a clear distinction between commands they found in Scripture and those they added in order to reinforce those commands. If you broke a scriptural command, you were liable for a sin offering, but no penalty was imposed if

---

3. Cecil Daniel Wray, *A Short Inquiry Respecting the Vestments of the Priests of the Anglican Church and Whether the Surplice or Black Gown Should Be Worn during the Sermon* (London: Joseph Masters, 1856) (TinyURL.com/GownOrSurplice).

you merely broke a rabbinic command.[4] In contrast, the church has made rules that are penalized by excommunication. Paul advised temporary exclusion for the most severe unrepentant sin, for example the person who was sleeping with his stepmother (1 Cor 5:1–5; 2 Cor 2:6–9). But in later centuries the church prescribed permanent exclusion for many lesser offenses. From the fourth century, church councils published anathemas, or curses, of excommunication on those who broke church rules. Even today, you can be excluded from the membership of some churches by missing too many Communions or by disagreeing with a particular doctrinal view, such as details about the second coming.

God's commands in the Old Testament are a precious revelation of God's purposes for us. They show us how to live, even in the harshest environment, surrounded by degrees of spiritual evil that (thanks to God's law) have now almost disappeared. Jesus showed us how to apply this revelation of God's purpose to different circumstances in a new generation. We should look for what God's purpose was and then find a practice that promotes that same purpose today. God's purposes don't change when our society changes, so we should seek to promote that purpose rather than the specific rules that revealed it.

We are now ready to deal with some real-life examples. The previous chapter provided a clear method for discovering whether a rule in the Bible applies timelessly to all cultures or was restricted to a particular time and place. If a rule is changeless throughout the Bible and is also countercultural in at least part of the Bible, we should conclude it is timeless. This chapter has provided a method for dealing with rules that aren't timeless: we can reinterpret them for today by looking for the original

---

4. E.g., Mishnah *Shabbat* 6:1–4 (TinyURL.com/Shab6-1).

purpose of that rule. This summary makes the task look easy, but we will find two questions keep cropping up:

1. What *was* the culture at the time that this rule was given in the Bible?

2. What *was* the original purpose of this rule, which now appears to be senseless?

Both questions often require researching details of ancient history. However, in order to interpret these details, we need to imagine what it was like to live at the time, given what we know about the lifestyle of those who lived then and human psychology. Often the best way to do that is to imagine how we would feel and act if we were in their place. This means that you don't need to be an ancient historian to make useful contributions in this type of investigation.

Section 2

▼

Children

4

▾

Abortion and Infanticide

In Bible times, babies were killed just after birth instead of just before.
Newly converted Gentile Christians were given only four absolute
moral prohibitions—including a condemnation of this practice.

I helped deliver twelve babies when I was a medical student—an extraordinary experience. And I also watched a healthy but unwanted baby being broken up and sucked away in a late-term abortion—sickening. Later that same day I attended an infertility clinic. It was full of hopeful but mostly sad couples, any of whom would have been overjoyed to take that baby home. I didn't complete medical training (my doctorate is in New Testament history) so I never had to decide whether I would opt out of that work that no doctor enjoys doing: helping people kill their unwanted babies.

In New Testament times there were just as many unwanted babies as today. This was due to poor birth-control methods and a sexual free-for-all that makes modern societies look prudish. Abortion was rarely practiced, because it was dangerous for the mother. Instead, the solution to the problem of an unwanted child was infanticide—the baby was born normally and then killed. In Roman society the final decision on whether a child lived wasn't made by the mother, but by the head of the household—usually the mother's father, if she wasn't married.

Every newborn had to be laid on the floor before him, and the custom was that if he picked it up and named it, the baby lived. If not, the child would be "exposed."

The word "exposed" became a euphemism like the modern word "abortion"—which originally referred to the natural ejection of a fetus that was too malformed to survive birth. The term "abortion" is so consistently misused as a euphemism for killing an unborn infant that doctors now have to talk about "spontaneous abortion" when they mean natural abortions. In a similar way, "exposed" originally meant leaving an unwanted baby on a hillside for the child's fate to be decided by the gods. Perhaps a kindly stranger would rescue the baby, or even—as in the story of the twins Romulus and Remus, who founded Rome—a kindly she-wolf. In practice, the infants died, though some were "rescued" by brothel keepers as a future investment.

When Roman life became urbanized, this rural practice became difficult. Rather than someone trying to covertly leave a crying infant in a quiet street, the baby would be smothered before being thrown out. Philo, a first-century Jewish preacher, fearlessly criticized this Roman practice: "With monstrous cruelty and barbarity they stifle and throttle the first breath which the infants draw."[1]

FOUR NEW RULES

When Gentiles became Christians, they had to learn a whole new lifestyle, just as a modern convert may have to adopt new standards of sexual morality or stop swearing. The first church council (described in Acts 15) decided that Gentiles didn't need to be circumcised (whew!), but they did need a crash course on morality in four essential areas. The council summarized the

---

1. Philo, *Special Laws* 3.114, trans. C. D. Yonge (TinyURL.com/PhiloSpecial3).

prohibitions in just four memorable and pithy words (which aren't so pithy in translation): idol offerings, sexual immorality, blood (i.e., bloodshed, or possibly eating blood), and something called *pniktos* (on which see below). They sent this list to all the new Gentile churches, together with representatives of the council to explain what each one meant. Unfortunately, this explanation wasn't recorded for us to read, which has resulted in some confusion.

The first three would be recognized by all Jews as the three most heinous sins: idolatry, sexual immorality, and bloodshed. Jews regarded these as "mortal sins" because they believed that any of God's laws could be broken if life was in danger—your life or someone else's—except for these three laws.

Gentiles thought differently. Idolatry was what glued Roman society together—you made friends by joining in whatever religion they enjoyed in their variegated cosmopolitan culture. Sexual immorality was officially frowned on, but the number of brothels and the affairs reported by contemporary social commentators suggests Roman morality was very flexible. Sex with slaves, for example, was not regarded as reprehensible because this was part of a slave's natural duties. Even bloodshed was a normal part of Roman lifestyle—as a spectator sport when gladiators fought to the death, or as the right of any slave owner if he wished to "dispose" of his property.

But the fourth prohibition—the word *pniktos*—is mysterious, because the word is so rare. Bible translators up until now have assumed it meant something similar to the related verb *pnigō*, "to strangle," suggesting something like "strangled meat." However, strangling was not a normal way to kill animals—birds' necks were broken, and it is very hard to strangle a sheep or an ox! For an academic study I looked up every occurrence of *pniktos* in the whole of ancient Greek literature on a massive computer database.[2] There are only twenty instances before the third century AD, and every author except one used it as a specialist culinary term that could best be translated as "smothered meat." This wasn't meat smothered with sauce—it referred to baby animals who were smothered as soon as they were born. This was done to produce the tenderest meat possible, rather like an extreme version of suckling pig.

Of course, the new Christians weren't being warned to avoid this particular expensive delicacy—that would be like telling believers that one of the four worst sins is eating *pâté de foie gras*! (However, I expect that they *would* avoid this food, just as many Christians tend to avoid eating veal, because of the way it is produced.) In the context of the other three mortal sins, this prohibition of "smothering" is clear: "Do not smother babies." Like the three other sins, infanticide was common and acceptable in the Gentile world, but it was absolutely abhorrent to Jews and Christians.

Interestingly (though admittedly irrelevant), the one ancient author who used *pniktos* differently was an engineer called Heron of Alexandria in the first century BC. He invented the steam engine and the self-emptying cistern almost two thousand years before James Watt and Thomas Crapper. These modern engineers applied their inventions to moving heavy objects and making toilets flush. But Heron's patron had slaves to do all the heavy and dirty work. So Heron's steam engine made mechanical singing birds move around his patron's garden fountain, and his cistern dispensed wine in limited quantities for his patron's alcoholic son. His inventions needed airtight joints, which he

2. For more detail, see my article "Infanticide and the Apostolic Decree of Acts 15," *Journal of the Evangelical Theological Society* 52 (2009): 301–21 (TinyURL.com/Acts15-Infanticide).

described as "smothered" (*pniktos*) joints. This helps confirm the meaning of this rare word and also shows how the world might have progressed faster without slaves.

Back to the church council: They sent representatives to explain the meaning of these four words—these four prohibitions—and to urge all believers to memorize them (Acts 15:27). They were very successful: the early church stood out in the ancient world as people who rejected idol worship, sexual immorality, bloodshed, and infanticide.

FULL HUMAN RIGHTS

Forbidding abortion and infanticide is therefore an example of a countercultural command. In the prevailing Roman culture, the normal practice was infanticide—killing babies as soon as possible—and abortion is simply doing that a little sooner. There is no command against infanticide in the Old Testament, though people sometimes point to the law about the loss of a baby when a pregnant woman was accidentally struck (Exod 21:22–23). This certainly shows that an unborn life was regarded as having the same value as a person, because the maximum penalty in this case was death. But it doesn't say anything about deliberate abortion. However, in the case of countercultural commands, we don't need to show that the command is unchanging—we should presume it is timeless because God has asked believers to act differently from those in the surrounding culture.[3]

In the past, the law regarded children as the property of their parents, with limited rights before adulthood. Modern society has learned, largely from Jesus, that children have full human rights, and their vulnerability makes us especially responsible for looking after them. However, somehow we've managed to

---

3. See chapter 2, "Finding Fixed Morals for a Changing World."

concede that a fetus is not a child, so it's not due the same legal protection. Perhaps this is because churches have so often condemned those who are accidentally pregnant instead of offering to help take care of the child.

The successful change in the status of children was not imposed on society by making laws. The laws reflected a change that had already occurred in UK society, led by the church. The eighteenth-century church provided free general education for the poorest children on Sundays, which was the only day when they didn't work; and they opened orphanages for street children. This was the origin of Sunday schools, which later promoted religious training when all children had gained the right to free weekday schooling.

Perhaps the way to change society's views about abortion is not by demanding stronger laws but by continuing to provide adoption agencies and accommodation, care, and advice for those who are facing the crisis of an unplanned pregnancy. Often these are the most vulnerable in society. As with all those whose lives are in a mess, if we can show Jesus' love to them and their unborn children, society will hopefully realize that life itself is precious, even before it is born.

5

Rebellious Children

Paul disqualified church leaders whose children were disorderly. Unlike Roman parents, we are no longer responsible for legally punishing crimes by those in our household. So what is our role when children rebel?

I remember the day when I resolved never again to say: "I blame the parents." My four-year-old daughter was having a tantrum, lying on her back, screaming at the top of her voice, in the aisle of a crowded shop. I was unable to quiet her, and she was struggling so much that all I could do was drag her along the shiny floor by her ankle, to the evident disapproval of several clucking women. It was when she conceived the clever idea of grabbing hold of the base of a shelving unit that I made my resolution.

Paul wrote to Timothy, who was a pastor in Ephesus, that someone who can't keep charge of his own family should not lead the church: "He should manage his own household well ... keeping his children submissive" (1 Tim 3:4 ESV). He tells Titus, who pastored on Crete, that the children of church elders should not be "open to the charge of being wild and disobedient" (Titus 1:6). According to some translations the children even had to be "believers," but the old King James Version catches the nuance of the Roman culture better: they had to be "faithful," because *pistos* implies someone who could be trusted to pay for goods and honor legal agreements.

Does this mean that Christian leaders should resign if their children go off the rails? My daughters are both very sensible, but there is still time, as my wiser friends tell me! What if they do go through a late rebellious phase—would I have to give up positions of church leadership?

We know from historical sources that Crete had a particular problem with their youth. They were wildly promiscuous, and it seems that the youth of the church were also afflicted with this (see Titus 2:4-6).[1] And we know from modern-day life that the pastor's kids are often the worst! However, in Ephesus, there may have been a bigger problem with older men, because the main library (the ruins of which are now a popular tourist attraction) was opposite the largest brothel, and a secret tunnel connected them.

When Israel followed the Old Testament law, rebellion by children was theoretically impossible. The law about obeying parents was in the top ten: "Honor your father and mother so that you may live long in the land the LORD your God is giving you" (Exod 20:12). This sounds like a promise, but actually it was a threat. The penalty for a "stubborn and rebellious" son who ignored parental discipline was death by stoning (Deut 21:18-21). The rebellion could have included all kinds of bad behavior, so the Bible (as it normally does) lists the lowest offenses in order that anything more serious will be automatically included. For rebellion against parents, the offenses it lists are gluttony and drunkenness (Deut 21:18-21).

---

1. See Bruce W. Winter, *Roman Wives, Roman Widows: The Appearance of New Women and the Pauline Communities* (Grand Rapids: Eerdmans, 2003), 163-65.

We can understand that drunkenness is serious, because it is often accompanied by violence and uninhibited behavior that can lead to almost anything. But why was gluttony included? In an agrarian society that relied on an annual harvest and careful rationing of that food until the next harvest, a glutton could bring starvation to a family. This wasn't the case for every family, of course, but if necessary a child could be removed for the sake of the whole family. A terrible decision! We don't know whether this punishment was carried out very often; probably there was no need to.

A similar attitude was found in other ancient civilizations, including Roman culture, which had spread throughout the world by the time of the New Testament. The head of a household in Roman law (the *paterfamilias*) was responsible for every member of his family and for any slaves he owned. If any of them committed a crime, he was legally expected to be their judge, jury, and executioner. In theory he could literally execute them if their crime deserved it, though he could send his child into exile as a legal alternative. The responsibility of the head of a household for punishing miscreants and criminals in his charge was treated very seriously. Anyone who let a child or a slave get away with their crime was threatening the fabric of society and possibly the safety of others. If they didn't apply the law, then no one else had the authority to do it, so the criminal would go unpunished and might commit a worse crime next time.

EMBARRASSING TEENAGERS

The emperor Augustus led a moral crusade throughout the Roman Empire shortly before Jesus was born. For example, he decreed that adultery had to be punished by death or exile, and the responsibility for carrying out the sentence lay with the head of the household.[2] Augustus portrayed his own "first family" as a model for the empire to emulate. Then disaster struck: his own daughter Julia was found to be prostituting herself just for the thrill of doing something forbidden. And then his granddaughter Julia the Younger became pregnant in an adulterous affair. Even if they both repented, Augustus couldn't let them off because everyone would assume that either he was a hypocrite or that the law didn't really matter. So, when the baby was born, he had it exposed (i.e., killed), and he exiled them both to live on separate small islands, devoid of any luxury, and never saw them again.

Heads of households were responsible for punishing other crimes, too. Damage to property, theft, personal injury, and even murder had to be judged and punished by the *paterfamilias*. Nowadays it would be illegal for a father to punish his children in this way. Some immigrant subcultures in the West still follow similar customs that they brought with them from their countries of origin. These customs create complex legal problems, which tabloid newspapers tend to portray in terms of child abuse. But in the first century it was illegal for anyone *except* the head of the household to inflict punishment.

Therefore, a father in New Testament times who couldn't or wouldn't manage his household when his children or slaves broke the law was a threat to society. His refusal to punish was a social evil as serious as a father who lies in court or covers up sex abuse perpetrated by his son. A man who did this would clearly be disqualified as a church leader, both then and now. As Paul said: "He must ... have a good reputation with outsiders" (1 Tim 3:7) — and someone who protected his child, to the detriment of society, would be rightly criticized.

---

2. *Lex Iulia de Adulteriis Coercendis* of 17 BC (TinyURL.com/WikiLexJulia).

A modern rebellious teenager is very different! Parents might do everything in their power to teach their children about the faith, to help guide them through life, and, where appropriate, to punish them. And yet they may still rebel. This isn't due to parental failure, and it isn't what Paul was talking about. Paul wasn't saying that a rebellious child proves their parents can't lead. After all, God himself is a Father who has a whole planet full of rebellious children, and that situation doesn't reflect badly on him.

Paul was warning against choosing a church leader who had failed to carry out the legal responsibilities that he had in that culture. Someone who failed to carry out these legal duties was not just a poor parent but also a threat to society—and he himself was breaking the law. Of course, it is also true that parents who do nothing to help, guide, or reprove their rebellious child are likely to be poor leaders and are certainly a poor example to others. But the true situation is usually difficult to evaluate from outside the family, and we should be very reluctant to judge others.

MAKE THEIR OWN MISTAKES

These Bible commands about dealing with children are not changeless, and they are culture reflecting, so we can't assume they should apply in all cultures. Parents should not stone their rebellious drunken children (as the Old Testament commands), and pastors should not lose their leadership positions for failing to "manage" their children (as the New Testament commands). Both of these commands reflect the culture that these believers were living in. In New Testament times, Christians were expected to follow the Roman law that made them legally responsible for their own households. And in Old Testament times there were no prisons where a dangerous drunk could cool down, and there were no police or full-time soldiers to enforce an injunction keeping a violent person from a vulnerable family member.

Also, this law changed over the time the Bible was written. By New Testament times the Old Testament command was no longer observed, though everyone still knew of it. Jesus' enemies glibly charged him with breaking this command when they said he was a "glutton and a drunkard" (Matt 11:19 = Luke 7:34), but they made no attempt to carry out any punishment. Times had changed, and the law was no longer enforced. This shows it was not a changeless law that applies to us today. And the equivalent, though different, law in the New Testament that fathers must legally manage their household also applies differently in a different culture.

Ultimately, in any culture, children have to make up their own minds, and sometimes we have to let them make their own mistakes. Our task, as parents, changes as they grow. The toddler we guide turns into a child we instruct, a teenager we reason with, and finally into a young adult with whom we discuss problems. We love them and pray for them, but they can still go astray. Sometimes, sadly, we can trace the rebellion of children back to the attitudes and actions of their parents. But ultimately every young adult is an individual who is free to choose the way to live. As God said in Ezekiel 18, children don't inherit guilt from their parents' sins, and similarly parents do not bear the ultimate guilt for their children's rebellion.

6

▼

Childlessness

The Bible appears to be full of miraculous babies, but there is also childlessness. Unlike other literature of the time, the Bible doesn't blame the parents, but recognizes their sadness. Jesus proposed a solution that helps but doesn't remove the sadness.

The problem of infertility is as old as the hills, and there are few issues that cause more ongoing pain. Modern medicine can help in many ways, but often the journey is agonizingly long and ends fruitlessly. Sometimes medicine can destroy relationships by ascribing the "fault" to one partner. And although relationships can grow stronger through this trial, they can also be brought to a loveless end of unspoken recriminations and regrets.

The Bible doesn't appear immediately helpful for those who long to have a child, especially as the first recorded command is "be fruitful and increase in number" (Gen 1:22). Another problem is that it seems as though every barren woman who cried out to God for a baby had her prayers answered. However, when we look closer, we find that isn't so. During the thousand years from Abraham to David, the Bible recounts the lives of several families in remarkable detail. But in all this time we find only six childless women whose prayers for a child are answered: Sarah had Isaac; Rebekah had the twins, Jacob and Esau; Leah had Reuben and four other sons; her sister Rachel had Joseph and Benjamin; Hannah had Samuel; and an unnamed mother had Samson. And in the rest of the Bible, only one more is documented: Elizabeth, mother of John the Baptist. These seven women had their stories recorded because the sons they gave birth to grew up to be famous. Presumably there were many more childless women throughout this period, and I'm sure they all prayed for a child. Some had their prayers answered, and some didn't—but they aren't listed because their children are not historically significant.

SADDEST WOMAN IN THE BIBLE

One childless woman in the Bible was the sad second wife of Moses—an Ethiopian woman we know almost nothing about, except that she was probably the most reviled and loneliest woman in the Bible. She lived in the shadow of Moses' first wife, Zipporah—an independent and strong woman—and she had to put up with rejection by Moses' family. His brother and sister, Aaron and Miriam, even organized a public protest against her.[1] To cap it all, Moses' new wife had no sons, a matter of public disgrace (in 1 Chr 24:15 the only sons of Moses are Zipporah's). Even if she'd had daughters, she would still have been regarded as childless in Old Testament times, because without a son the family name died.

Childlessness was a disgrace in ancient times because everyone assumed it was a punishment from God—a silent reprimand for a secret sin. Who could deny that they had done something wrong at some time? It was an explanation that the whole of the ancient world agreed with. Although Hannah and Elizabeth were able to praise God that their disgrace was ended (1 Sam 2:1;

---

1. See more details in chapter 19, "Racism."

Luke 2:25), most childless couples had to simply suffer the rumors. All the ancient literature that mentions childlessness assumes that it is due to sin, with one significant exception: the Bible.

The Bible never lays any blame on those who are childless. It doesn't imply, suggest, or insinuate that childlessness is a punishment. Childless couples are portrayed as innocent, sorrowful, and loved by God. The Bible understands the agony of the childless, listing them along with the destitute as those who are to be most pitied, the opposite of the rich and happy (1 Sam 2:5; Isa 54:1).

Childlessness in the Bible can be a consequence of situations ascribed to God, such as warfare or famine, but there is no indication in the Bible that God *uses* childlessness as a punishment for sin. It is portrayed as one of the "normal" things we suffer in this fallen world, like illness and premature death. The Psalms even acknowledge that God gives children to the wicked (Ps 17:14), just as he blesses both the good and evil with sunshine (Matt 5:45). This message is so different from anything else written at the time—shouted so loudly—that we can't escape its conclusion: God loves childless couples.

Probably the hardest Bible verse for childless couples is Psalm 128:3 because it says the faithful are fertile: "Your wife will be like a fruitful vine." This can come across in English as a promise of children, but translating Hebrew poetry into another language is just as difficult as translating English poetry. The problem here is the Hebrew imperfective tense: it is usually translated as "will ..." (i.e., future), but it can also mean "may ..." (i.e., subjunctive or jussive). Because this psalm consists of blessings, ancient Hebrew readers would have understood this verse as "May your wife be fruitful like a vine"—that is, "will be" isn't a prediction but a blessing or a prayer. The Bible is full of God's blessings for health, food, and fertility, but it doesn't pretend that God's people will always escape illness, hunger, or childlessness in this world spoiled by sin.

In Jewish culture, childlessness was doubly devastating because ancient Jews took the command to have children very seriously. The rabbis even ruled that a man who hadn't had a child by the tenth year of marriage should divorce his wife and marry someone else in order to have children. One childless woman, who evidently loved her husband very much, went to the rabbi Simeon ben Yohai—a famously strict rabbi living soon after New Testament times. She hadn't had any children after ten years of marriage, and she didn't want to lose her husband. Simeon tried to cheer her by saying that she could have a wonderful party before she left and choose anything she wanted from the house, however valuable, and take it with her. So she organized a party with lots of wine. And when her husband was drunk, she tipped him into a wheelbarrow and trundled him out of the house, because he was the only thing she wanted to take! The improbably happy ending to this story is that Rabbi Simeon realized how much this woman loved her husband, and he allowed them to stay together.

WAS JESUS BREAKING THE LAW?

Jesus loved the company of children, but his singleness meant that he could never have any of his own. He had to address this command to have children because he was evidently breaking it. He said that it was permissible for people to be "eunuchs for the sake of the kingdom" (Matt 19:12). He didn't mean to castrate yourself, and he made sure his listeners didn't think this by first listing the two standard categories of eunuchs as defined in rabbinic law: a eunuch made by others and a eunuch from birth.[2] Jesus' third category was a eunuch "for the sake of the kingdom." Paul also followed this path by remaining celibate in order to avoid the practical responsibilities of supporting a wife and bringing up children (1 Cor 7:25–28).

The command to have children is not a timeless one because it is clearly different in the Old and New Testaments. This is a clear signal that the command in the Bible doesn't apply to all cultures because, of course, it has already changed within the span of the Bible.

Jesus' permission to deliberately avoid marrying and having children is countercultural because Jews insisted on following the command in Genesis, and the emperor Augustus decreed that all Romans should have children—and gave financial and legal incentives in his law, the *Lex Julia* of 23 BC. Countercultural commands are especially significant because believers are asked (or in this case, invited) to do something that goes against the norm for the culture they are in. This makes Jesus' teaching especially significant and likely to apply to all cultures.

This certainly makes sense when we look at the world we live in. At the time when Jesus revoked the command to fill the earth, there were already people all over the world, though not nearly as many as today. The job of filling the earth was clearly going well, and today we can declare: job done!

The purpose behind the original command was literally to fill the earth. Humans were just starting out, and they needed to have lots of children—especially due to the sad fact that so many of them died. In Jesus' day, they could relax somewhat. The Romans still encouraged childbirth because they wanted a bigger army, but it didn't really matter whether a proportion of the human race opted out of having children. And today, we can

---

2. Mishnah *Zabim* 2:1 (TinyURL.com/Zabim2-1).

see that the purpose behind that command has been fulfilled, and there is no need for everyone to follow the Old Testament command any more.

However, the big issue today is not whether we *have to* have children, but whether we *can*. Jesus understood the feeling of emptiness experienced by the childless and taught the church how to help by putting a new twist on Psalm 113:9: "He gives the barren woman a home, making her the joyous mother of children" (ESV). Jesus said that in his kingdom, believers should share what they have. That way, those who lack a home, or belongings, or children will gain them a hundredfold, though "with persecutions" (Mark 10:29–30). Although sharing each other's families may not completely fill the emptiness of child-lessness, it can help. Believers can share what they have with others in the kingdom, though they will still have "persecu-tions"—in other words, it will help the pain, but only so far.

There are only a small number of miraculous babies in the Bible, but for those who can't have one, they can appear to be everywhere—just as the streets they walk along seem to be full of parents with children. Being an informal aunt or uncle to a friend's child may not be easy for those desperate to have chil-dren themselves, but it is a wonderful way to be involved with them. And having another adult to love and be interested in chil-dren can bring great benefits for them and their parents. Our Lord has set us in the family of the church, and our nuclear-family barriers should be low enough for our children to clamber over and bless the lives of those without children of their own.

7

Should Girls Be Educated?

An educated woman in New Testament times was regarded as haughty and most probably immoral. Christians therefore had to be circumspect about educating women. If Paul and Jesus hadn't encouraged this, would the church be like the Taliban?

It's amazing to think that my daughters will have more opportunity to enter the career of their choice than at any other time in history. All I have to worry about is that they will choose wisely. For the first time, too, women can expect to progress in most professions without needing to emulate men; they can employ their skills and personality with true equality. It is easy to look down on other societies where things are less equal, but things were very different in the West until fairly recently. Across the road from my office is Newnham College, which was established for girls in 1871 despite protests. Cambridge University reluctantly allowed women to attend university lectures so long as they didn't sit the exams.[1] Women were not awarded full Cambridge degrees until 1948, and they didn't make up 50 percent of the students until 2002!

In the Roman world of New Testament times, an educated woman was treated with suspicion. Sallust (a first-century BC

---

1. "History of Newnham" (TinyURL.com/NewnhamHistory).

Roman historian) wrote scathingly about a wealthy woman, Sempronia. She excelled in the social arts and in Greek and Latin literature, wrote poetry, conversed with wit and charm, and could "dance more adeptly than any respectable woman would have needed to. ... She took the initiative with men far more frequently than they did with her."[2]

The only women who were expected to have an education were the *hetairai*—the high-class call girls. They had to be sophisticated and educated in music, dance, coiffure, and other "feminine skills." The most highly sought-after *hetairai* also studied philosophy, literature, and other subjects, which made them capable of intelligent conversation with their clients. A generous host would provide expensive *hetairai* for his guests not only for after-dinner "exercise," but also to contribute knowledgeably to the discussions during the meal.[3] Wives weren't traditionally invited to accompany their husbands on these occasions—they were expected to wait demurely at home. But things were changing.

During the first century a women's liberation movement was gathering steam. Women gained new legal rights, including the authority to spend their own money how they wanted without their husband's permission. They began to be educated in areas that were normally the reserve of men and attended parties alongside their husbands. Unfortunately, the movement was distasteful to most people because some women began to demand equality with regard to taking lovers (such as Sempronia, described above), so the movement became associated with immorality. It was normal for men to have lovers

2. Sallust, *The War with Catiline* 25, trans. Judith Peller Hallett, in Sarah B. Pomeroy, *Goddesses, Whores, Wives, and Slaves* (New York: Schocken Books, 1975, 1995), 171–72.

3. For more on *hetairai* see TinyURL.com/HetairaUC.

or sleep with slaves whenever they wished, but a woman faced divorce if she spent even an evening away from home without permission. All that changed when rich women started to openly pursue famous gladiators or poets—and then boast about their conquests. The most infamous example was Messalina, the wife of the emperor Claudius. She (allegedly) summoned the entire Praetorian Guard to attend her high-society ladies' party and organized a competition to see who could have sex with the most men.

WOMEN'S LIB

These "liberated" women misused their freedom and brought suspicion down on anyone who spoke up for equality of the sexes. Any woman who wanted equality was assumed to be immoral, and because of this even education was thought to be dangerous. The father of Seneca (a Stoic at the start of the first century AD) said that education made a woman lazy and vain.[4] Rabbi Eliezer (a very conservative rabbi at the end of the first century AD) said, "If you teach your daughter the Scriptures, you might as well teach her to be sexually immoral."[5] In other words, even seemingly good education will corrupt women. Today we find this logic difficult to understand, though we see the same thinking among the Taliban, who burn down girls' schools to defend morality as they see it.

In the first century, the new Christians had a problem: they believed in equality at a time when this was potentially scandalous. They believed in the equality of slaves and free men, which was bad enough, but even worse, they also believed that men and women were equal (Gal 3:28). The danger was that if

4. Seneca, *Ad Helviam* 17.3 (TinyURL.com/AdHelviam).
5. Mishnah *Sotah* 3:4 (TinyURL.com/Sotah3-4).

they proclaimed this too loudly, it could confirm the general belief that Christianity was "an abomination ... a most vile superstition ... hideous and shameful" (as the Roman historian Tacitus described it).[6]

Given all this, it was amazing that Paul allowed women the right to pray and prophesy in public meetings (1 Cor 11:5). In the Jewish world women did not even pray at the dinner table at home, let alone lead prayers in a synagogue; in the Roman world, prayers were spoken by a priest or the highest-status male who was present. And as well as the radical step of permitting women to pray aloud in public, Paul also, controversially, allowed them to attend teaching meetings and gain an education. This was unheard of. One indication that this wasn't normal lies in the name of the room in which teaching or symposia normally took place—it was traditionally called the *andron*—that is, the "men's room."

Paul did draw the line, though, at allowing women to speak out during teaching meetings (1 Cor 14:35). This was a bridge too far that would not have been accepted in those times under any circumstances. Speaking out, even under the guise of asking for information, would have been regarded as contributing to the teaching process. This was especially the case in Jewish and Roman societies, where so much teaching consisted of asking a pupil questions to reinforce what they had learned. His response, that women should ask their husbands at home, is identical to that of Plutarch (a first-century AD moralist), who said: "If they do not receive the seed of a good education and do not develop this education in company with their husbands they will, left to themselves, conceive a lot of ridiculous ideas and

---

6. Tacitus, *Annales* 15.44 (TinyURL.com/TacAnn15-44).

unworthy aims and emotions."[7] In other words, Paul is telling them to follow the Roman customs and stop stirring up trouble in a public meeting.

As modern readers, we don't notice the barbed way in which Paul recommends education for women in 1 Timothy 2:12–14 by sarcastically criticizing the lack of it. On first reading he appears to put the blame squarely on Eve for being deceived when Adam wasn't. But Paul also reminds the reader of the reason why she was deceived: Eve was not there when God explained to Adam about not eating the fruit (in Gen 2:16–17)—she had not yet been created. The implication is that Adam didn't do a very good job of teaching Eve about what God had said and, because of that, the serpent was able to deceive her. Paul also implied that Adam was doubly guilty: first for failing to teach God's command properly to Eve, and second for joining in with her sin even though he knew better. Any intelligent man would have felt a pang of conscience reading this because, in refusing to educate women, they were repeating Adam's mistake. In plain language, Paul blamed men for the fact that women were likely to have little understanding and were therefore more liable to commit sin through ignorance.

AT JESUS' FEET

Jesus was also in favor of educating women, though this wasn't part of his public message. When he was a guest at the house of Mary and Martha, he used the time as a teaching session for his disciples. We know, of course, that Mary sat down with the disciples to listen to him, but it is difficult for us to appreciate how forward and presumptuous this would have seemed. Women

---

7. Plutarch, *Advice to the Bride and Groom or Moralia: Conjugalia Praecepta* 48 (TinyURL.com/PlutarchEducate).

were not supposed to seek education—and certainly not along-side men. Martha ignored it at first, perhaps in the hope that Mary was just dawdling there temporarily, but when it became clear that Mary was deliberately including herself among Jesus' pupils, Martha lost her temper. We can imagine everyone sud-denly noticing Mary and looking at her with shock and undis-guised disgust, but Jesus stood up for her. He was happy that Mary had chosen to learn and even called it the "better" path (Luke 10:38–42).

If Jesus had spoken only in synagogues, he wouldn't have been able to reach women very well. But instead he preached outside—anywhere—in the Gentile area of the Temple (where the women and money changers were allowed) and even on isolated hillsides. When the thousands were fed, they included "men … women and children" (Matt 14:21; 15:38). Women even followed Jesus around to help and presumably to learn, like the disciples (Matt 27:55; Luke 8:3; 23:49, 55).

There is nothing in the Old Testament about educating women. This was partly because very few people indeed were given any form of education. The practice of writing may have been widespread, as indicated by the multiple pottery shards bearing people's names, which presumably indicated ownership. But the phonetic alphabet they used could be learned in a couple of hours, so this didn't require a formal education system. It was only merchants who needed more lit-eracy in order to understand contracts and accounts. We should assume the ideal wife described in Proverbs 31 had this higher level of learning because she traded in cloth and land. But only senior civil servants such as Daniel would have been given a proper education.

So it is difficult to decide whether there is any timeless com-mand about whether to educate girls. The command doesn't need to occur in the Old Testament, and it is relatively minor in the New Testament. The more important issue is, like in some cultures today, mixed up with whether girls and boys are equal. And on that matter Paul is clear: "There is neither Jew nor Gentile, neither slave nor free, nor is there male and female, for you are all one in Christ Jesus" (Gal 3:28).

No one today would argue that the Bible teaches women should not be educated. After all, Paul says "a woman should learn"—though we must admit that the full sentence is "A woman should learn in quietness" (1 Tim 2:11). However, it was a close call—it would have been so easy for Paul to ban teaching women like he banned them uncovering their heads.[8] Why did Paul go against his upbringing in Judaism and against the Roman culture by allowing women to learn? There is nothing in the Old Testament to tell him that women should be educated. His most likely source is the Gospel traditions that were circulating. If it hadn't been for the example shown by Jesus, the church might have, like the Taliban, refused to educate girls.

Of course, the medieval church appeared to backtrack on this, because they only actively taught men. But this was a matter of culture rather than policy. Nuns were encouraged as much as monks to read and meditate on Scripture, though being a scribe was considered a male job. In a similar way, children of rich parents were given tutors, though there was more incentive to educate males, who would use knowledge to earn money. But that didn't stop young princess Elizabeth (b. 1533) learning enough to read Erasmus's newly printed New Testament in Greek. The church laid the foundations so that when society could afford it, education was available for girls as well as boys.

---

8. See chapter 27, "Jesus' Effeminate Hair."

Section 3

▾

Sex and Marriage

8

▼

Sexual Immorality

Can a converted sexual hedonist ever feel clean again? Most New Testament converts came from a more licentious lifestyle than a porn star. They found a solution.

When I was a teenager a friend told me about an embarrassing experience of "evangelism." His church decided that the best way to attract new members was to stand and sing on the church steps. Predictably, they were largely ignored, but then a "lady of the street" who was walking past stopped to look up at them. My friend climbed down to give her a printed invitation to the church. When he returned to the group he was met by a scowling elder and the reprimand: "We aren't looking for *that* sort of member."

Ancient Jews were much more horrified by sexual immorality than even the most conservative Christian today, but if early Christians had separated themselves from anyone who was sexually immoral, the church would have grown very slowly. In Roman society, boys were encouraged to experiment sexually from a young age—at about fourteen years, parents gave them a ring of manhood that was often engraved with an erect phallus. It is unlikely that any male got married as a virgin—though, hypocritically, all girls were expected to be virgins when they first married.

Prostitutes were everywhere. Corinth, for example, was a sailors' city, with all the amenities they demanded and a reputation to match. But it was not much better elsewhere because most Roman cities emulated the vices of their capital. In the ruins of the upper-class provincial town of Pompeii, where many rich Romans had their holiday villas, there are twenty-six buildings that appear to be brothels—one for every sixty homes. Prostitutes were found even in morally principled Palestine, especially after the Roman soldiers began their occupation shortly before Jesus' birth. Jesus wasn't just being metaphorical when he called his contemporaries an "adulterous and sinful generation" (Mark 8:38), and we shouldn't be surprised to read in the Gospel accounts that prostitutes were among his listeners.

INTERNAL FILTH

The Pharisees were particularly aghast when Jesus ate with "tax collectors and sinners" (Matt 9:11). Tax collectors were bad enough—they had collaborated with the occupying army in return for a rich lifestyle. But much worse were the "sinners." These were women, and perhaps boys, whom the tax collectors provided for the "pleasure" of their dinner guests, just like their new overlords the Romans did. While most Jews strenuously avoided contamination with anyone or anything they regarded as sinful or impure, Jesus mixed with everyone. He wasn't concerned to keep himself ceremonially pure and didn't even worry about preserving his reputation. He loved people from all walks of life and wanted to show them the love of God. Jesus told the Pharisees their concerns about physical impurity were misdirected because sin does not originate from external contamination, but "evil thoughts ... sexual immorality, theft, murder, adultery ... come from inside" (Mark 7:21–23).

Jesus wasn't trying to annoy these religious leaders. He was trying to shame them into repentance. Those people whom they called "sinners" did at least recognize their need for forgiveness, and large numbers did repent. The early church contained many who had been grossly sexually immoral. Because it was the normal sexual lifestyle of Roman society, those who weren't sex workers themselves had probably been their clients. Almost every New Testament letter warns against sexual immorality because of the many believers who could easily slide back into their former habits.

What did the church do when believers fell into sexual sin? In serious cases, such as the believer who was sleeping with his stepmother, they were expelled from the fellowship (1 Cor 5:1–5). However, this wasn't permanent—Paul urged the Corinthians to let the excluded member back in after he'd had time to repent (2 Cor 2:5–7). Many other believers in Corinth were guilty of sexual sin, but thankfully to a lesser degree. Paul reminded them that the "sexually immoral [and] adulterers" are not part of the kingdom and then said: "That is what some of you were, but you were washed and sanctified and justified in the name of the Lord Jesus Christ" (1 Cor 6:9–11). Jesus had forgiven them, and that was good enough for Paul. Nevertheless, a few verses later he has to remind them that visiting prostitutes is wrong now that they are Christians (vv. 15–20).

A ONE-WOMAN MAN

In contrast to ordinary believers, church leaders had to be totally free of sexual sin. The young evangelists Timothy and Titus were warned not to appoint anyone who was in love with money, alcohol, violence, or sex, and Paul said that a leader should be (literally) "a man of one woman" (1 Tim 3:1–12; Titus 1:6–9). This phrase was a male version of the Latin *univira* ("one-man"), which was commonly used to describe faithful wives. No one but Paul used this male version of the phrase—it would have been nonsensical because almost no Roman male could or wanted to be described as a one-woman man. In ruling that Christian leaders should be unfailingly faithful to their wives, the church was therefore making a dramatic stand.

Can sexual sin be totally forgiven? King David discovered that sexual sin can have endless consequences—he sent Bathsheba's husband to certain death at the most dangerous part of the front line. But David also found forgiveness through painfully sincere repentance, as Psalm 51 testifies. There was also room for repentance when Israel committed "adultery" with other gods. Even after God was forced to divorce her because of her persistent refusal to stop being unfaithful, he still urged her to repent and offered to marry her again (Jer 3:1–14; 31:1–4; Isa 62:4–5).

Neither the Old nor New Testament puts blame on sex workers themselves. The enticing wayward woman of Proverbs is criticized, but she is a married woman (Prov 5:1–20). However, temple prostitutes (the *qedeshah*) aren't criticized, though those who sell women into this trade and the men who used them certainly *were* criticized (Deut 23:17; Hos 4:14). Former sex workers were accepted back into society, and any Israelite, including a religious Levite, could marry one. It is true that a priest couldn't marry a prostitute—but then he couldn't marry a widow or a rape victim either, so this had nothing to do with any guilt perceived in the woman (Lev 21:7). Rahab was described as a "prostitute" (*zanah*) in Joshua 2:1, 6:17, and (in case the reader has forgotten) in 6:25. According to Jewish tradition, she later married Salmon, the grandfather of King David, and she is named in the genealogy of Jesus (Matt 1:5).

Both Testaments therefore have the same commands to avoid sexual immorality, and in both cases this was countercultural.

The ancient Near Eastern world and Roman society were even less concerned about sexual immorality than modern Western society, as far as men were concerned, though of course wives had to remain pure. In Israel and the church, both sexes were expected to follow a path of sexual purity, though both fully accepted someone who repented. That this command is changeless and countercultural means that it is timeless.

WHAT TO DO WITH OFFENDERS?

The church has been rightly castigated for its many sexual scandals, which we now recognize have occurred because the command against sexual immorality has not been followed. Checks on church workers and volunteers now enforce the vigilance that should have been present before. However, this new climate can also make us much less accepting of offenders, even if they truly repent. Just as offenses remain on a register, they remain as a permanent blot on someone's record. This can make us reluctant to accept people with a questionable history, even in a church that preaches forgiveness.

It is vital that we protect our children and vulnerable adults from predators, but it is also vital for the church to recognize the possibility of genuine repentance and new life. Accepting someone with a history of sexual sin into our church is no different from welcoming someone who repented from fraudulent business practices or repeated dangerous driving. They can all reoffend, and the responsibilities we do or do not give them need to reflect that possibility, but with sensible guidelines and willing cooperation on both sides there is no reason why past convictions should marginalize people in God's family.

God was willing, as a husband, to forgive even the gross, repeated adultery of Israel. He promised not only to forgive her, but even regard her as if it had never happened, because the prophets say that he wanted to marry her as if she were a virgin again! (Isa 62:1–5). He has not only commanded forgiveness after immorality, but demonstrates that his forgiveness is unlimited toward those who repent.

9

▼

Homosexuality

The Bible strongly condemns same-sex hedonism and changing one's sexuality. What would it have said about same-sex faithfulness practiced today and about people born different?

I feel that I should "come out" and admit that I am a nonpracticing adulterer. What I mean is that I am married, but I'm still attracted to other women, though I don't act on this impulse. I'm far from alone in this condition, and I'm guessing that this admission won't exclude me from any church positions. But what if instead I declared that I am a "nonpracticing homosexual"? This would be a much more difficult admission to make, and many churches would rule me out for leadership positions and wouldn't invite me to preach. Some churches would exclude me from membership, and I may feel uncomfortable even *attending* some churches.

What is the moral difference? In neither case am I acting on my inclination, so why is one regarded as reprehensible in some way? Why is it acceptable to be attracted to a woman other than my wife, but not acceptable to be attracted to a man? Yet many churches that would be willing to have an ex-adulterer as a minister would not consider having a homosexual person, even if he said he had always been celibate. This cannot be regarded as a moral stance; we should recognize that this is homophobia.

The Bible clearly condemns homosexual practice (Lev 18:22; 20:13), though it does not condemn homosexuals. In contrast, the nations surrounding ancient Israel despised homosexuals but only outlawed homosexual practice if it involved rape.[1] The Middle Assyrian code from the fourteenth century BC contains a very insightful law concerning homosexuality:

> A#19 If a man furtively spreads rumors about his com-
> rade, saying, "Everyone has sex with him," or in a quar-
> rel in public says to him, "Everyone has sex with you,"
> and further, "I can prove the charges against you," but
> he is unable to prove the charges and does not prove the
> charges, they shall strike that man 50 blows with rods;
> he shall perform the king's service for one full month;
> they shall cut off his beard; moreover, he shall pay 3600
> shekels of lead.[2]

This law shows that homosexual behavior was shameful—because making this accusation without proof was punishable as slander. If the accused had been proved guilty of adultery, he'd face the death penalty. However, no punishment is prescribed for the accused person if proof is presented that he did indeed sleep with other men. So it wasn't illegal, though most considered it shameful.

We don't have any evidence in the Old Testament that those with homosexual inclinations weren't shunned, though the

---

1. Robert Gagnon has collected all the ancient literature in *The Bible and Homosexual Practice* (Nashville: Abingdon, 2001).

2. Translation based on the *Assyrian Dictionary of the Oriental Institute of the University of Chicago*, ed. Martha T. Roth (Chicago: University of Chicago Oriental Institute, 1964–2010), and *The Context of Scripture: Canonical Compositions, Monumental Inscriptions and Archival Documents from the Biblical World*, ed. William W. Hallo (New York: Brill, 2003), 2:355.

lack of something rarely proves anything. However, the rabbis, who constantly imbibed and lived the Hebrew Bible, made the following rule, which suggests they weren't homophobic: two unmarried men may not sleep together under the same cover.[3] This rule shows that they knew very well that some men were attracted to other men rather than to women. They also saw that the law condemned these activities, but this didn't make them try to identify and exclude this type of person from their community. They simply ruled that *all* unmarried men should avoid situations where such men might be tempted—without making any implications or accusations about specific individuals. Of course, this wasn't foolproof, because some would get married anyway to hide their inclination, but it was a sensible proportionate safeguard without any homophobic discrimination.

GREEK FASHION

The New Testament was also countercultural in this area. Paul condemned something that he called *arsenokoitēs* (literally "man-lying")—a word that didn't exist in Greek at the time (1 Cor 6:9; 1 Tim 1:10). It is formed by merging two words in the ancient Greek translation of Leviticus: "If a *man lies* with a male ..."[4] Like all Jews, Paul condemned homosexual practice on the basis of the Old Testament. But contemporary Greek and Roman culture didn't regard it as illicit—though most Romans looked down on those who practiced it.

Paul had an uphill struggle trying to convince Gentiles that homosexual practice was immoral. Alexander the Great had publicly taken his male lover with him on military campaigns and promoted him to second-in-command of the army.

---

3. Mishnah *Qiddushin* 4:13 (TinyURL.com/Qiddushin4-13).

4. *Arsenos koitēn* is the Greek Septuagint translation of Lev 20:13.

Consequently, long-term homosexual relationships became fashionable in Greek society and were regarded as more intimate than the business of making legitimate heirs with one's wife. It isn't surprising that many Romans—who regarded Greeks as highly cultured—emulated this lifestyle.

However, Roman society was much more interested in hedonistic homosexuality than long-term relationships. Conscientious dinner hosts provided boys as well as girls for recreation after all-male dinner parties. This was supported or tolerated by most Romans, though some philosophers criticized it as a mere quest for titillation to spice up jaded sexual palates.

Some forms of homosexual practice were beyond the pale even for Romans—in particular, being a passive (i.e., penetrated) partner. Romans would penetrate a male slave, but it was regarded as degrading and humiliating for a Roman citizen to let himself be used in this way. Someone who allowed this was called *malakos*—effeminate or soft. When the emperor Nero married his long-term lover, Roman society wasn't shocked by the fact that his lover was male, but because the lover was an ex-slave and even more because Nero wore a bridal dress. This implied that he was the penetrated partner, which was beyond all Roman decency.

Lesbianism was also totally unacceptable. It was so far off limits that it is almost never mentioned in Greek or Roman literature. The only known case is the poetess Sappho, who lived in about 600 BC on the Greek island of Lesbos (from which we get "lesbian"), but the hints about her sexuality weren't recognized in her poetry until the nineteenth century. Like Queen Victoria, people didn't like to think that such things happened. Interestingly, Jews were well aware of women who, in rabbinic language, "rub against each other."[5]

---

5. Babylonian Talmud *Yebamot* 26b (TinyURL.com/Yebamot26b).

CLEVER TACTICS

Paul decided to exploit this inconsistency in Roman attitudes toward male and female homosexual practice. At the start of his letter to the Romans, where he wants to show that everyone has sinned, he used this to trick Gentile readers into acknowledging that they too had sinned. First, he condemned women who "exchanged natural relations for unnatural ones" (Rom 1:26). We can almost hear the Roman reader draw in a breath of shock that such things would happen. Having gotten their attention and agreement, Paul then tripped them up by continuing: "In the *same* way the men also abandoned natural relations with women and were inflamed with lust for one another" (v. 27). By pointing out the similarity between what women and men were doing, he trapped his Roman readers: if they agreed that female homosexual practice was unnatural, then the same must be true of male homosexual practice.

Paul used the same tactic in 1 Corinthians 6:9 when he listed two types of homosexual partners. He first names the *malakos* (the passive partner) which, as I've already said, was unacceptable for Romans themselves. Paul followed this immediately with *arsenokoitēs* (the active partner or the one who penetrates), which was perfectly acceptable in Roman morality. Putting the two side by side highlighted Roman hypocrisy in this matter and made the reader realize that if one practice was unacceptable, then so was the other. It is the same technique as a modern environmental campaigner might use: "We condemn those who continue to cut down rare hardwood trees and those who build kitchens out of them."

Was Paul writing about the same kind of homosexual practice that happens today? Human inclinations are unlikely to have changed much in just a couple of thousand years, so we must assume that people had the same kinds of inclinations then as now. Romans knew that some men were only attracted to men, and there were also men who copulated with anyone or anything during drunken orgies and even when they weren't drunk. Plutarch had a genteel way of describing those whom we'd now call "exclusively homosexual"—he said that "some men cannot mount their mare."[6] That is, even if they married, they couldn't do the business. Jews also knew that if a man wasn't married by age twenty, it was safer not to let him share a blanket with another man, because his inclinations may not have been directed toward women.[7] However, Paul wasn't describing someone like that.

We know that Paul wasn't describing men who can't be aroused by women because he says that they "exchanged" natural relations for unnatural, and "abandoned natural relations with women" (Rom 1:26–27). These men changed from having relations with women (probably lots of them) to having those same relations with men—and they probably changed back again, too, perhaps during the same party. These were men who would be universally regarded as degraded, perhaps even by themselves.

It was necessary for Paul's argument that every reader would condemn them. If they didn't do so, they wouldn't realize their own guilt when he concluded: "Although they know ... that those who do such things deserve death, they not only continue to do these very things but also approve of those who practice them" (v. 32). Every Gentile addressed by Paul's letter was guilty—not

---

6. Plutarch, *Moralia: Conjugalia Praecepta* 8 (TinyURL.com/PlutarchEffeminacy).

7. Mishnah *Qiddushin* 4.13. I discuss this further in "Evidence of Non-Heterosexual Inclinations in First Century Judaism," in *Marriage, Family and Relationships: Biblical, Doctrinal and Contemporary Perspectives*, ed. Thomas A. Noble et al. (London: Apollos, Inter-Varsity, 2017), 138–54 (TinyURL.com/Inclinations1stCJudaism).

of doing these things, but of approving those who practiced them. They didn't condemn the orgies that Paul referred to—they either attended them or envied those who did. The most debauched parties were organized by the richest and most powerful men in Rome, whom everyone had grudging respect for.

Today, this kind of behavior is much more democratized. Anyone can book a hedonistic holiday or attend a party where no social conventions are followed. Anyone can have a fling, chasing any kind of sexual fantasy or fetish on the internet or in the flesh. And if someone finds out and criticizes, they are labeled as a prude or judgmental.

WHAT DID PAUL CONDEMN?

According to the tests that I use throughout this book, the Bible's teaching on homosexuality must be timeless. Both the Old Testament and New Testament teaching was counter-cultural because contemporary societies did not outlaw homosexual practice. So the command that God is giving to believers shouldn't be expected to change in different cultures. And the command against homosexual practice does appear to be consistent through the Bible, especially as the New Testament terminology (*arsenokoitēs*) is based on Leviticus 20:13.

However, we should not shy away from asking what precisely Paul and the Old Testament were condemning. As we saw when we looked at Romans 1, it is easy to jump to conclusions that are wrong. It may well be that the other texts (1 Cor 6:9; 1 Tim 1:10; the prohibitions in Leviticus) refer to something different from what is condemned in Romans 1, but what is it precisely? We can't argue that Paul referred only to homosexual rape like that at Sodom, because he condemns both those who penetrate and who are penetrated (*arsenokoitēs* and *malakos*, respectively, in 1 Cor 6:9). However, there still remains a wide spectrum of homosexual behavior, from hedonistic bisexual promiscuity to lifelong committed same-sex partnerships. That the word *arsenokoitēs* was coined in the New Testament makes it very difficult to determine exactly what it refers to.

Some interpreters are more certain than I am about identifying precisely what Paul condemned. My inclination is to bring a practicing homosexual to Jesus, like they brought the woman caught in adultery (in John 8:2–11). Those people clearly wanted Jesus to condemn her to be killed by stoning, but he declined. I'd like to think that I'd be among the first to drop my stone and walk away—leaving the person with Jesus.

10

▾

Sex during Singleness

The rabbis, like most religious leaders, warned against masturbation. James Dobson, who has guided a generation of parents, regarded it as merely the practice of releasing "hormonal pressure."[1] What does the Bible say? Actually, nothing!

I was watching *Friends* with my daughters when a great romantic moment occurred. Chandler, who had been living with his girlfriend Monica for several months, finally came to a point of commitment. For the first time in their relationship he declared: "I love you." I switched to full alert as I realized this might be an opportune moment to say something like: "They've got it all backward, haven't they, girls? Love comes first, then marriage, and *then* sex." Just as I opened my mouth, both my offspring turned to me and chorused: "Yeah, Dad, we know." I guess I might have covered this subject before!

The boyfriend who doesn't want to commit is not just a fictional stereotype; and since the advent of contraceptives, an increasing number of girls have comparable reservations. And this isn't new. In first-century Roman society, young men tried to remain unmarried as long as possible. It wasn't that they couldn't decide who to marry—good parents chose a bride for

---

1. See TinyURL.com/DobsonOnMasturbation.

them—they just wanted to avoid marital responsibilities and the obligations of fatherhood as long as possible. Shortly before Jesus was born, Emperor Augustus made laws that rewarded young Romans for marrying and having children. He wasn't worried about the decreasing morals of the younger generation, but he *was* worried about the decreasing number of trueborn Roman citizens.

BROTHELS EVERYWHERE

Men had little incentive to marry, because sex was easily available outside marriage, and it wasn't expected that you would be able to marry someone you were in love with. Brothels were numerous, though there's some dispute about the numbers. Early excavators at Pompeii interpreted carvings of an erect phallus outside a building as an advertisement for a brothel. However, they found so many of these, along with extremely explicit erotic wall paintings, that the number of supposed brothels rose to one for every forty-five men.[2] Actually, these symbols were probably considered good luck charms, so not all of them pointed to a brothel. But this symbolism is telling in itself: a society that pays artists to create such explicit images on their walls is clearly relaxed about sex.

Such sexual freedom was considered extreme sinfulness in the Jewish and Christian world, though they still faced just as much temptation. Paul warned the young Timothy to avoid shameful things and to "keep a strong curb … on your youthful cravings" (2 Tim 2:21–22, a great translation by Weymouth).[3] He assumed that young women faced the same temptations and

---

2. See David Fredrick, ed., *The Roman Gaze: Vision, Power, and the Body* (Baltimore: Johns Hopkins University Press, 2002), 151.

3. Richard Francis Weymouth, *The New Testament in Modern Speech* (New York: Baker & Taylor, 1903).

that young widows would be particularly tempted because they weren't restrained by having to preserve their virginity. He therefore encouraged them to remarry to prevent them giving in to their sexual desires—that is, become pleasure-loving widows (1 Tim 5:6, 14).

Paul is often thought to have been against marriage, but this conclusion is based on only one passage (1 Cor 7), which includes an encouragement to delay marriage "because of the present crisis" (v. 26)—probably the worldwide famine that was underway at the time. As he reminds his readers, since marriage entails providing material support for your family (vv. 32–34), getting married and bringing children into the world during a famine was best avoided. Nevertheless, even in this difficult situation, Paul listed two reasons why it might still be better to marry your intended partner. First, you might feel that you were acting badly toward your betrothed—who might not be equally willing to wait for marriage (v. 36)—and second, your singleness might lead you into sexual sin (v. 9).

Paul wasn't against remaining single—he himself was single and recommended it. Jesus, too, taught that singleness was a valued choice made by some people who wished to serve the kingdom in a special way (Matt 19:12). But Paul recommended singleness with an important caveat—he pointed out that it was a "gift" that only some people have (1 Cor 7:7).

BURNING WITH PASSION

Paul speaks about sexual frustration in surprisingly vivid terms, saying, "It is better to marry than to burn" (1 Cor 7:9). This probably reflects the belief of Greek doctors that if a man did not release semen regularly, it would cause a harmful rise of temperature inside him. Going to a prostitute was therefore regarded as a normal, and even healthy, thing to do. That's why

Paul not only warned Gentile converts against visiting brothels, but even had to explain *why* it was an unacceptable practice for a Christian (1 Cor 6:9–20). Even the author of the book of Hebrews, which was written to a Jewish congregation, had to remind them that sex should only occur between married partners (Heb 13:4). Presumably the congregation was outside Israel, so they were constantly exposed to a culture that treated such things lightly.

Paradoxically, Paul didn't have to remind his converts that the Old Testament forbade sleeping with a girlfriend or fiancée. The law demanded "proof" that she was *virgo intacta* on her wedding night in the form of a bloody cloth. Lack of proof resulted in her death—her husband was unpunished because it was assumed he would not cause this, knowing the disastrous consequences (Deut 22:13–21). This may have reflected some inequality in cultural expectations, though warnings against extramarital sex were addressed to both sexes in Judaism. Paul didn't need to remind his readers of this because even Romans knew that women had to come to marriage as virgins. Somehow Romans didn't recognize the absurdity of expecting first-time brides to be virgins while grooms were expected to gain premarital "experience." Of course, this same double standard often still exists today.

Biblical teaching allows sex only within marriage, so what should unmarried believers do if they don't have the gift of singleness? This must have been a common situation among early believers because becoming a Christian made people unsuitable in the eyes of their intended in-laws. Even if they succeeded in finding a partner, they probably couldn't afford to get married because their non-Christian parents were unlikely to pay the dowry and other costs of getting married.

Today, too, many Christians find themselves unmarried—as do non-Christians. Romeo and Juliet's generation commonly married during their early teens, but today marriage takes place ten or twenty years after sexual maturity occurs. In this situation, it is not surprising that many non-Christians have sexual partners during those decades of singleness. What is surprising is that many young Christians succeed in heroically standing against this cultural expectation. It is very difficult to withstand sexual temptation at an age when your body is screaming for fulfillment and everyone around you is "doing it."

WHAT ABOUT MASTURBATION?

The earliest suicide counseling service, the Samaritans, was founded in 1953 by a London Church of England minister, Chad Varah, after conducting his first funeral service. He had to bury a fourteen-year-old girl who committed suicide after her first period, which she interpreted as a sexual illness. He vowed that he would provide help for all those whose ignorance about sexual matters caused severe suffering. This controversially included counseling masturbation for people who were overwhelmed by sexual frustration.[4] In today's secular society this advice is largely unnecessary, but is it appropriate for Christians? Some Christian leaders have bravely pointed out that "masturbation is not much of an issue with God" (James Dobson) and that "when someone is under pressure to the point of distraction ... it is often better that they relieve themselves" (Gerald Coates), though they also warn against letting it become a compulsion rather than just a periodic release.[5]

The Bible says absolutely nothing on the subject of masturbation, though most people assume it is banned. This silence is in contrast to the ancient rabbis, who even warned men to take

---

4. See, for example, TinyURL.com/ChadVarah.
5. These and others are cited at TinyURL.com/Masturba8.

care how they touched themselves while passing urine.[6] The story of Onan is often cited as forbidding masturbation because he "spilled his semen" (Gen 38:8–10). However, this Bible text criticizes Onan's refusal to carry out the ancient law that said that if a man died, his brother should help his widow conceive a son to look after her in her old age. Onan wanted to keep the whole family inheritance for himself, so he "spilled his seed" to prevent fathering a new heir to share the inheritance with.

What the Bible does warn against is fantasizing about someone. Job says, "I made a covenant with my eyes, not to look lustfully at a young women" (Job 31:1), and David's experience with Bathsheba shows what that can lead to. Jesus probably referred to this in his warning, "If your right eye causes you to stumble …" (Matt 5:29). These and other warnings against fantasizing are given because it can lead to immorality, though there is no specific warning against masturbation.

DELAYED MARRIAGE

The Old Testament did not have to give much warning against premarital sex, because there were no reasons to delay marriage. We have no accurate figures about actual practice, but later rabbinic culture probably reflects ancient practice. Most fathers arranged for their daughter's betrothal (a legally binding form of engagement) before she gained legal adulthood, at age twelve, to ensure she couldn't object. This was so common that the rabbis had to make a rule that girls could not actually be married before the age of twelve—so engagements tended

---

6. Rabbi Eliezer ben Hyrcanus, who lived just after Jesus, said: "He who holds his member while passing water is [as sinful as] one who brought a flood upon the world" (Babylonian Talmud *Shabbat* 41a [TinyURL.com/Shabbat41a]; *Niddah* 13a; 42b [TinyURL.com/Niddah13a]).

to occur when they were eleven and the marriage a year later.[7] Boys didn't marry until a little later, but the longer they waited, the more dangerous it became. There was a saying: "He who is twenty years of age and is not married spends all his days in sin."[8] One rabbi said: "The reason that I am superior to my colleagues is that I married at sixteen. And had I married at fourteen, I would have said to Satan, An arrow in your eye" (i.e., Satan couldn't have tempted him at all).[9]

The commands against sexual encounters outside marriage are unchanging from Old to New Testaments, though they are only countercultural in New Testament times. Ancient Near Eastern societies around Israel had just as strict laws forbidding adultery as Israel did, and they would have encouraged early marriage for similar reasons: to secure inheritance issues and to have maximum control over their children's choices. However, the rule of abstaining from sex before marriage was extremely countercultural for members of the early church and clearly caused a lot of problems. That this rule was nevertheless insisted on makes it clear that this is a timeless command.

Ideally, any believer who does not have the "gift" of singleness (as Paul puts it) should be able to marry someone whom they love and who will support them in the faith. But the modern lifestyle for young people interposes a prolonged period of education, and possibly occupational training, before marriage becomes practical, and many believers also have difficulty finding a suitable spouse. Many Christian men and women

---

7. If she was married before, she could annul the marriage when she became twelve (Mishnah *Yebamoth* 13.1 [TinyURL.com/mYeb-13-1]; *Niddah* 5.6 [TinyURL.com/mNiddah-5-7]).

8. Babylonian Talmud *Qiddushin* 29b (TinyURL.com/Qiddushin29b), attributed to Rabbi Huna in the mid-third century AD.

9. Babylonian Talmud *Qiddushin* 29b–30a (TinyURL.com/Qiddushin29b), attributed to Rabbi Hisda in the late third century AD.

therefore find themselves living what is, for them, a difficult and far-from-ideal life as a single person.

If someone is full of adrenaline from pent-up anger we might counsel them to hit a punching bag. Others have so much physical energy they need to go for regular runs to achieve any sense of calm. What should we say to those singles who suffer so much pent-up sexual energy that everyone they look at becomes an object of desire? Scripture warns us against acting on such desires, but does not condemn the release of such tension by masturbation. I realize that this is a difficult conclusion for many Christians who would regard masturbation as giving free rein to passions that they feel should be subdued by other means. But for some of those believers who do not have the gift of singleness, it may be a way to release their sexual frustrations while living a life honoring to God.

11

▾

Jesus Outlawed Polygamy

Jesus used the same Old Testament text to teach monogamy as used by the Jews of the diaspora and at Qumran. Polygamy had been useful in times of war for childless widows, but now it was causing hardship.

When an African tribal chief converts to Christianity, what happens to all his wives? Should he divorce them and send them back to their parents' home in shame and penury, or should he live away from them in a separate house, but continue to provide for them financially? This is a classic problem for missionaries in countries that practice polygamy, and one to which there is no easy answer—just the fervent hope that the next generation will marry only one wife! It must seem very strange for those polygamous families when their normal, socially acceptable lifestyle is suddenly regarded as immoral.

The Jews whom Jesus lived among had the same problem. Polygamy had been considered perfectly normal and proper until the Romans took over and said it was disgusting and immoral. The Romans allowed Jews to continue practicing polygamy in Palestine, but elsewhere in the empire monogamy was strictly enforced. Many Jews living outside Palestine therefore got used to the principle of one wife, and it seemed natural to them. By Jesus' time, many Jews had come to agree with the Roman view,

and polygamy fell out of practice during subsequent generations, although the Jews did not actually outlaw polygamy until
the eleventh century.

We don't know how frequent polygamy was among the Jews
in Jesus' day because we have the complete family records of only
one family in the early second century—they were preserved in
a bag hidden in a desert cave. So it is significant that this family
does include a second wife. The documents include the marriage
certificate of a widow called Babatha when she married a man
who already had a wife. Babatha owned her own land and business, so she didn't marry for financial support—perhaps it was
for companionship, or even love!

POLYGAMY IN THE BIBLE

The Old Testament allows polygamy but doesn't encourage it.
Great men such as Abraham, Israel, Judah, Gideon, Samson,
David, and Solomon had multiple wives, though the Old Testament records many problems that resulted. However, the law
actually made it mandatory in one circumstance: if a married
man died without leaving a male heir, his brother was required
to marry his widow regardless of whether he already had a
wife. This was so that she would have support during her old
age (either from her new husband or from her son) and so that
the family name and land would be passed on (Deut 25:5–6).
Polygamy was also allowed in other circumstances, and the
only restriction was that you shouldn't marry two sisters
(Lev 18:18). Polygamy was beneficial when the number of men
was reduced by warfare. It not only helped women who would
otherwise be on their own, but also helped to replace the population more quickly. In peacetime, however, this practice meant
that if rich men had more than one wife, then some poor men
had to remain single.

Jesus took the side of the Romans against the Jewish establishment on this occasion. Most Jews outside Palestine and some in Palestine disagreed with polygamy. For example, the Qumran sect regarded polygamy as one of the three great sins of mainstream Judaism. They called these sins "the nets of the devil" by which the "smooth-speaking" Pharisees entrapped the people.[1]

They couldn't actually find a verse in the Old Testament that spoke against polygamy, so they combined two different verses that both contained the phrase "male and female"—Genesis 1:27 and 7:9. The first says, "God created them; male and female," and the second says, "two and two, male and female, went into the ark" (ESV). Since "male and female" were called "two" in Genesis 7, the Qumran community inferred that it also meant "two" in Genesis 2 and concluded from this that only two people could marry. They referred to this doctrine as "the foundation of creation." We may not be convinced by their logic, but as far as they were concerned it was case proven.

Jews outside Palestine used a different method to show that polygamy was wrong—they added a word to Genesis 2:24. This says "a man ... is united to his wife"—which implies one man and one wife, so they emphasized this conclusion by adding the word "two" to the next phrase: "and those *two* shall become one flesh." We find this additional word in all ancient translations of Genesis—in Greek, Aramaic, Syriac, and even in Samaritan—showing that it had very widespread support. Presumably it also had some support among Hebrew speakers, but no one in Jesus' day would deliberately change the original text, so no Hebrew Bible has this word.

When the Pharisees were questioning Jesus about divorce, he took the opportunity to set them straight about polygamy

---

1. Damascus Document 5 (TinyURL.com/VermesScrolls, p. 316).

too. Jesus used both sets of arguments used by other Jews. He quoted the key verse used by Qumran Jews (Gen 1:27) and even said this was what happened "at the beginning of creation" (Mark 10:6, which presumably reminded his listeners that Qumran Jews called this "the foundation of creation"). Then he quoted the verse preferred by Jews outside Palestine— Genesis 2:24—including the additional word "two" (Mark 10:8; Matt 19:5). By deliberately using both arguments, Jesus emphasized that he agreed with those Jews who taught monogamy, contrary to the Pharisees.

Paul took the teaching against polygamy further by reversing the command that a man had to marry his dead brother's wife. This had always been a difficult rule, though it made sense in the world of the early Old Testament. In Hittite law (and probably other ancient Near Eastern laws), a widow could be married against her will to *any* male relative—even to her husband's elderly grandfather or infant nephew. But Moses' law restricted her marriage to someone of roughly her age—that is, she should only marry a brother of her husband—and she was allowed to refuse. Paul later decided that this law was outmoded. He said that a widow could marry whomever she wanted (1 Cor 7:39)—though he added that she should marry a fellow believer.

CREATING NEW PROBLEMS

Enforcing monogamy may have cleared away a scandal, but it created a new problem for the church. Suddenly there were more widows without husbands and without support because they couldn't become anyone's second wife. To try to help these widows, the church created a new type of social club for them—a widows' association. This spread outside Palestine as a good solution to a problem they shared, because no polygamy was allowed outside Palestine. It was one of the first things the fledgling church did, and right from the start it was problematic—Greek-speaking widows complained that the Aramaic speakers were being given more food, for one thing (Acts 6:1)! Young Timothy, leading the church in Ephesus, had other problems with his widows, and Paul had to write a whole chapter to help him cope (1 Tim 5). Nevertheless, this association was a good solution to their needs, and it was far better than expecting these women to each find a new husband.

Why did Jesus and Paul change God's commands? Had God always been in favor of monogamy so that they were now returning to his original wishes? Although Jesus said that this was how things were at the "beginning," this doesn't mean that God had subsequently given the wrong commands to Moses. It was the *purpose* of these commands, rather than the commands themselves, that was important. It was God's purpose that Jesus and Paul were upholding.

God's purpose for marriage was to help individuals find mutual support in families. When there were too few men due to warfare, this purpose was accomplished by allowing polygamy to ensure male heirs. In more stable times, polygamy resulted in many men remaining single because wealthy men could have many wives. In order to maintain God's purposes at times like these, the rule about polygamy had to change. God's purposes are eternal, but his commands change in order to carry out those purposes in different situations. We might summarize God's purpose in the words of Psalm 68:6: "God sets the lonely in families."

We can feel smug that our society doesn't allow polygamy, but in some ways we are like the Romans, whose law was based on a morality that most didn't follow. Despite their official condemnation of polygamy, many respectable Romans had multiple marriages because divorce was easily obtained and mistresses were openly accepted. Eurydice, a newly wed Roman wife in the first century, was given advice about a happy marriage by Plutarch: "If your husband commits some peccadillo with a paramour or a maidservant, you ought not to be indignant or angry, because it is respect for you which leads him to share his debauchery, licentiousness, and wantonness with another woman."[2] In other words, extramarital sex was so normal that she shouldn't take offense.

In modern Western societies, various surveys have revealed that 13 percent of women and 20 percent of men commit adultery[3]—and this is likely to be *under*reported by those who are questioned. Perhaps soap operas represent our society more accurately than we'd like to believe.

Jesus criticized polygamy as a warped version of the lifelong committed relationship of a one-plus-one marriage. Our society recognizes that this is a very special relationship, and we strive toward it, but in many cases we fail. So much time and money are often spent on the wedding and an almost equal amount on a subsequent divorce, but often we spend little time, care, and attention on the marriage itself.

---

2. Plutarch, *Moralia: Coniugalia Praecepta* 16 (TinyURL.com/Plutarch Peccadillo).

3. See Wendy Wang, "Who Cheats More? The Demographics of Infidelity in America" (TinyURL.com/InfidelityUSA), quoting the University of Chicago's General Social Survey.

12

▾

No-Fault Divorce

Jesus was asked about divorce for "any cause"—a type of no-fault divorce that was new and popular at the time. Jesus rejected it, but he didn't reject the Old Testament grounds for divorce: adultery, abuse, and abandonment.

I come from Brighton, which in my childhood was a popular destination for illicit lovers going away for a "dirty weekend." In those days it gave Brighton a rather risqué reputation. It also meant that a large number of private investigators operated in the town who could be hired to catch adulterers. As a teenager I had a perverse pride when I read yet another newspaper story about a divorce case citing a liaison in Brighton.

Paradoxically, many private investigators were hired by the man they were supposedly investigating. They'd be given the name of a hotel and a room number and be instructed to turn up "unexpectedly" at a certain time. The man would then hire a prostitute to sit in bed with him and call for room service at the prearranged time. When the maid brought the food she would see them both in bed, and the investigator would slip in behind her, armed with a camera.

This was common because fabricating evidence of your own infidelity was one of the easiest ways you could get a divorce. It was very difficult to obtain one for any reason except adultery, and this scenario provided two witnesses and photographic proof that could be used in the divorce-court case. But in 1969 divorce legislation was revolutionized on both sides of the Atlantic. In the UK, the Divorce Reform Act allowed divorce for anything considered to be "unreasonable behavior" that led to the "irretrievable breakdown" of the marriage. In the US, Ronald Reagan signed a bill that made California the first state to allow no-fault divorce; this eventually spread to every other state in the nation. Previously, in both countries only the wronged partner could file for a divorce, and it was only allowed for a specific set of grounds; now, even an innocent partner can be divorced against their will, albeit after some delay.

This significant change in divorce legislation was very similar to new legislation that became popular just before the time of Jesus. If we look at Jesus' teaching on marriage and divorce in context, we can see how best to apply it today.

MARRIAGE AS A CONTRACT

Every married Jew in Jesus' day had a marriage contract—some of these have been found in caves around the Dead Sea. These recorded the marriage vows and listed the money that both brought into the household, as well as detailing how much both of them would lose if they didn't keep their vows. English translations of the Bible tend to use the word "covenant" instead of "contract" for the Hebrew word *berith* (see Prov 2:17; Mal 2:14) because "contract" makes marriage sound too businesslike. However, only one covenant in the Bible has no penalties associated with breaking it—the wonderfully exceptional new covenant that God promised his people (Jer 31:31). All the other covenants in the Bible have stipulations, with penalties if they aren't carried out, just like modern business contracts.

The stipulations in a marriage are the vows, and the penalties are the divorce settlements.

The penalties prescribed for breaking marriage vows were mainly financial. In Jewish marriages just before Jesus' day, the groom promised that if he broke his vows he would return the dowry money plus a minimum of 200 *zuz* (about $20,000 in our money), so a poor person couldn't afford to get divorced. If the bride broke her vows, her husband would retain the dowry when they divorced.

If a marriage vow was broken, it didn't mean that divorce was compulsory; the wronged partner could decide whether to forgive or to divorce. However, in Jesus' day, some rabbis were starting to teach that divorce *was* compulsory for adultery. Jesus reminded them that Moses didn't "command" divorce; he merely "permitted" it (Matt 19:7-8). Jesus encouraged the wronged partner to forgive their spouse for the broken vows, though he didn't say how many times.

Many of the prophets envisioned Israel's relationship with God as a marriage, where God was a jealous and long-suffering husband and Israel was an adulterous wife who worshiped other gods. God eventually decided to "divorce" Israel by sending her into exile and threatened to do the same to the sister nation of Judah. God is therefore described as a divorcé by Jeremiah and Isaiah (Jer 3:8; Isa 50:1).

Malachi recorded that God hates divorce. This doesn't mean that God hates *divorced people*; rather, he hates the treachery and breaking of vows that lead to divorce (Mal 2:14-16). In fact, no one knows the pain of divorce more than God himself, who suffered the infidelity of his "wife," Israel, for hundreds of years.

When Jesus taught about divorce, he reminded his hearers about God's relationship with Israel by using the word "hardhearted." This word was invented by the Greek translators of the Old Testament and wasn't used in everyday Greek, so anyone who used it was quoting an Old Testament text. It occurs only twice in the Old Testament (Deut 10:16; Jer 4:4), and the second instance is in a passage about God's divorce from Israel (Jer 3–4).

In choosing to use this particular word, Jesus was therefore deliberately reminding his listeners that God didn't "divorce" Israel until the point when she was sinning "hardheartedly"— that is, stubbornly and continually. His conclusion, then, is clear—we should attempt reconciliation before considering the option of divorce.

In making this point, Jesus actually digressed from the question he'd been asked, because he wanted to talk about marriage, not divorce. He reminded his questioners that marriage was a lifelong commitment by which Adam and Eve could live together forever in perfect harmony. But then sin came along, and Jesus recognized this by saying that God introduced divorce because of "your hardheartedness." He wasn't saying that only his contemporaries were sinful—"you" refers to everyone. Human nature is still the same now, and Christians as well as Jews can be hardhearted. Jesus explained that because of our sin, God *allows* divorce.

But that doesn't mean divorce *should* happen. If someone had asked Jesus how many times one should forgive broken vows, he would have said seventy-times-seven times (Matt 18:21–22), because this is how many times God forgave Israel.[1] In the end, even that marriage ended, but the divorce itself wasn't the sin— divorce is always the result of the sinful breaking of marriage vows by one or both partners.

---

1. 2 Chr 36:20–21—they were exiled for seventy years so the land could catch up on the seventy Sabbath-year rests it should have had, which means that Israel neglected God's law for the last seventy-times-seven years.

BURNED DINNER

The problem in Jesus' day was that many men wanted easy divorces. God's law allowed a man to divorce his wife if she broke her marriage vows, but some wanted a divorce when there were no valid reasons for it. One group of rabbis (the Hillelites) resolved this "problem" by inventing a new form of easy divorce. We would probably have called it a no-fault divorce, but the term they used was "any cause" because of the Bible text they based it on.

They derived this new type of divorce from Scripture using an ingenious legal maneuver. Everyone agreed that the strange phrase "a cause of nakedness" in Deuteronomy 24:1 meant "adultery." But the Hillelites argued that the word "nakedness" by itself implies adultery, so the word "cause" must have *extra* meaning. Moses, they claimed, must therefore have been referring to *two* grounds for divorce: "a cause" *and* "nakedness." They concluded that "nakedness" meant divorce for "adultery," but "a cause" meant divorce for "any cause"—and thus they created the new law of divorce for any cause.

Actual examples included a single burned meal in one case, and in another a wrinkle on the wife's face that she didn't have when her husband married her[2]. Divorces such as these were, in effect, what we now call no-fault divorces. This new law was completely different from the Old Testament laws for divorce that the Jews cited in their marriage contracts, which contained marriage vows (based on Exod 21:10–11) that promised a supply of food, clothing, and love, as well as faithfulness (based on Deut 24:1).

By the time of Jesus most Jews had adopted this new law, including the two most prolific Jewish authors of the day, Philo and Josephus. In fact, they both talked about "divorce for any

---

2. Mishnah *Gittin* 9:10

cause" without reference to any other grounds for divorce that existed.[3]

Although most Jews used and accepted the new any-cause divorce, it was still a topic of heated debate. One group of rabbis in particular, the Shammaites, stood vehemently against it. They said that "a cause of nakedness" was a single phrase so it only referred to one ground for divorce. They summarized their position by saying that Deuteronomy 24:1 referred to no ground for divorce "except for sexual immorality" (i.e., adultery). They therefore rejected the Hillelites' any-cause divorce.

This was the context for asking Jesus: "Is it lawful to divorce one's wife for any cause?" (Matt 19:3 ESV). Jesus answered by agreeing with the Shammaites—that is, defending the traditional interpretation of the text—and he even quoted their slogan that Deuteronomy 24:1 referred to no ground for divorce "except for sexual immorality" (Matt 19:9).

Most modern readers misunderstand this question. Unless you know about the any-cause divorce, you'd think they were asking Jesus whether he approved of divorce in general. This is understandable, because legal jargon is often confusing. Imagine someone who has never heard of a no-fault divorce and comes across it for the first time. They might imagine that the divorce has happened because one partner is so annoyingly and tediously faultless. When you read legal jargon as plain language, it can be very confusing!

In Jesus' day, everyone knew this legal jargon because everyone was talking about the new any-cause divorce. It was such a hot topic that Mark didn't even bother to include these words. He records the question to Jesus as: "Is it lawful for a man to divorce

---

3. Philo, *Special Laws* 3.30 (TinyURL.com/PhiloSpecial3); Josephus, *Antiquities* 4.253 (TinyURL.com/JosephusAnyCause).

his wife?" (Mark 10:2). Worded like this, the question is actually nonsense—of course divorce is lawful, because it says so in the law. Imagine someone asking, "Is it lawful for a sixteen-year-old to drink?" This question is equally nonsensical, because without any liquid a person will die. It only makes sense to us because we mentally add the words "any alcohol"—because this is the common question of the day. Similarly, Mark's readers would mentally add the words "for any cause"—because that's what everyone was discussing.

However, once the debate was over and the any-cause divorce had become the only type of divorce available, the technical term "any cause" was forgotten very quickly. It's rather like the English concept of "divorce by co-respondent" that was frequently cited along with lurid details in the popular newspapers of my youth. Nowadays most people have forgotten what it means. It sounds as if you can be divorced for having a pen pal, but actually a "co-respondent" is someone you commit adultery with—look it up in a good dictionary. This was once a commonly known legal term, but it is now as unremembered as "any cause" was by the second century.

HOW DOES THIS APPLY TODAY?

Is the law about divorce timeless, or does it change with one's culture? We might conclude that the law changed between the Old and New Testaments, which would suggest that it is not timeless. However, as we have seen above, this is based on a misunderstanding. Jesus affirmed divorces based on adultery, and he vehemently criticized the Hillelites, who wanted to change the interpretation of Deuteronomy 24:1.

Faithfulness wasn't the only marriage vow. As mentioned above, Jews also promised to feed, clothe, and love each other, based on the law of Exodus 21:10–11. This wording gradually morphed into "love, nourish, and cherish" (based on Eph 5:25, 28–29) and then into "love, honor, and cherish." Those who neglected their spouse could be divorced—male or female— and this included abandonment or abuse, which were regarded as worse cases of neglect. This explains the scriptural basis for Paul's conclusion that an abandoned spouse is free to remarry (1 Cor 7:15). Unfortunately, both Jews and Christians moved away from this interpretation in the second century when they both forgot the origins and meaning of the any-cause divorce.[4]

This means that the church was left with an unworkable divorce ethic, where partners were locked into abusive marriages. The UK and US governments have consequently abandoned their Christian foundation and introduced no-fault divorces, which are, in effect, exactly what Jesus was rejecting. He wanted no divorce unless there was a specific ground based on broken marriage vows. Believers should not, of course, break their marriage vows, so in theory a pair of believers would never be divorced.

But in practice, Christians commit adultery, abandon or abuse their spouses, or even get divorced when no vows have been broken. We should take care that the victims of divorce aren't regarded in the same way as those who break their vows because, after all, God is a divorcé. But also we should not regard divorce as a minor matter, given that Jesus was clearly against the breaking of marriage vows.

---

4. For more information on this, see my *Divorce and Remarriage in the Church* (Downers Grove, IL: InterVarsity Press, 2003), readable at www.instonebrewer .com/DivorceRemarriage/DRC.

13

▾

Marrying Nonbelievers

Many in the Old Testament married non-Jews, but Paul clearly forbade marrying nonbelievers—perhaps because all Romans had to share the religion of their spouse. Does this rule still hold today?

I took a lot of girls out when I was at university. I had to. Matchmaking was a common hobby in the Christian Union, so as soon as a couple went out more than twice, their friends started planning the wedding. It was embarrassing for everyone, and I was determined it wouldn't happen to me. I devised a cunning plan: I decided that every time I went out, I would take a different girl. It seemed to work well ... until I met that special person. She was not interested in me because I was obviously far too shallow! Happy ending: she married me eventually.

The Christian dating process is abnormal in many respects. Even if you enjoy clubs and pubs, you're not likely to meet many Christians there, and you don't meet many new people at church or work. This means that the Christian social scene at a university or college can become a frantic hunt for a partner. Otherwise, you are left trawling through internet descriptions trying to discern the real Christians from those who prey on such sites. A significant number of Christians remain single against their wishes because they have not met a suitable Christian partner. For them, the command that Christians should only marry

Christians can be one of the hardest in the Bible. Others marry non-Christians and can face criticism from fellow believers because of this.

CAUSING A SCANDAL

If a New Testament believer married a nonbeliever, this would have caused a scandal both inside the church and outside, because in the Roman world, a husband and wife had to share the same religion(s). If a Roman woman married into a family that honored different gods, she had to worship them too. If she didn't, their children could not be Roman citizens.[1] In some ways, all Romans followed the same religion—the emperor cult—and they could also venerate whatever other gods they wanted. In Plutarch's advice to newlyweds, he tells the wife to worship her husband's gods,[2] but this merely means that she added his gods to the ones she already venerated.

This wasn't a big issue in Roman society, where it was a virtue to honor all gods, but it was a huge problem for Jews. To make sure they weren't pressured to worship other gods, Jews were only allowed to marry other Jews. Their divorce certificates reflected this by saying: "You may now marry anyone you wish, but only a Jew." The additional phrase "but only a Jew" was actively discussed in the early centuries, so presumably this had been recently adopted because of this Roman cultural attitude.[3]

Being of the same religion was especially important when children came along. How could both parents go to the temple,

---

1. Susan Treggiari, *Iusti Coniuges from the Time of Cicero to the Time of Ulpian* (New York: Oxford University Press, 1993), 44–50.

2. Plutarch, *Moralia: Conjugalia Praecepta* 19 (TinyURL.com/PlutarchGods).

3. The text is "not a heathen" in Mishnah *Gittin* 9:2 (TinyURL.com/mGittin-9-2); it is "Jewish man" in the divorce certificate found at Masada (see my *Divorce and Remarriage in the Bible* [Grand Rapids: Eerdmans, 2002], 120 [TinyURL.com/MasadaGet]).

make an offering, and get the priest's blessing for their child if they worshiped different gods? This is probably why the Corinthians worried that children of mixed marriages hadn't been "sanctified." Paul assured them they didn't need to worry—God himself sanctified their children (1 Cor 7:14).

All this means that we shouldn't be surprised when Paul clearly says that believers should not be "yoked together with unbelievers" (2 Cor 6:14). Although this phrase could possibly perhaps refer to a business relationship in this context, it is unlikely. Greeks and Jews normally referred to marriage as a "yoke" and called a divorce "unyoking," even in legal documents. Elsewhere, Paul is unambiguous when he says "she is free to marry anyone she wishes, but he must belong to the Lord" (1 Cor 7:39)—using the Christian equivalent of the Jewish phrase we saw above: "but only a Jew." He is addressing widows in this passage, but there's no indication that other believers are different in this respect.

Christian teaching on mixed marriages, therefore, reflected Jewish teaching in its effort to fit in with Roman culture. However, it was different in one important aspect: Christians weren't allowed to divorce a partner simply because they had a different religion. Paul said that Jesus' teaching on lifelong marriage applied *just as much* to mixed marriages as to marriages between believers. Like most early churches, there were couples in the Corinthian church where only one partner had become a Christian, and some of these believers felt that they should divorce their nonbelieving partners. But Paul taught that marriage vows were lifelong in God's eyes, and divorce should not be sought without biblical grounds. He told one woman who'd already left her husband to return to him if he was willing to have her back (1 Cor 7:10-11). However, some believers had been divorced against their will by their nonbelieving partners, probably because they refused to worship in pagan temples. Paul told those believers that they could regard this Roman divorce as a valid release from their marriage (1 Cor 7:15).

Does this teaching about marrying only Christians apply today? A timeless command is one that doesn't change through the Bible and doesn't tend to reflect the culture of its time. So is this command in agreement with the Old Testament?

JESUS' FAMILY TREE

We might at first think that the ancient Jews were taught to marry only fellow believers, because kings are told not to marry multiple wives or foreign princesses who might entice them to another religion (Deut 17:17). Individual Jews, however, married foreigners without any hint that this was wrong, though they were not allowed to marry women from the enemy nations of Palestine (Josh 23:12). For example, Moses married two foreigners, a Midianite and a Cushite (Exod 18:1–2; Num 12:1); and two of the three women named in Jesus' genealogy were foreign—Ruth and Rahab were Moabite and Canaanite, respectively (Matt 1:5; Ruth 1:22; Josh 2:1; 6:24). It wasn't until Ezra's time that there was a campaign to prevent intermarriage with all foreigners (Ezra 10:2, 10–14), and legal formulas forbidding such marriages are not found on any documents before Jesus' day.

In fact, the restrictions imposed on marriage in the Old Testament appear to be tribal, not religious. A woman who owned land could only marry within her own tribe, so that her land was not lost to other tribes (Num 36:8–9). And when Abraham decided his son Isaac should not marry one of the surrounding Canaanites, he didn't send his servant to find fellow worshipers of Yahweh, but to find someone from his family tribe (Gen 24:3–4). Although Rebekah's family referred to "Yahweh," this was only *after* they'd heard Abraham's servant use the name of his God (24:26–27, 31). Her family actually worshiped local family gods, like the people they lived among; Laban was Rebekah's brother, and we see him worshiping "household gods" in 31:19. So her religion was of secondary importance to Abraham, because he could assume she would adopt Isaac's religion. His chief concern was that Isaac married someone from among his tribal group.

Our second test is whether this command was simply reflecting the culture of the time. Endogenous marriage (that is, marriage within tribal groups) was very common in the ancient world, and it is this that created and maintained the distinctiveness of different tribes and nations. Marrying within the same religion was also important, and even more so in New Testament times. So the rules about intermarriage were certainly influenced by the cultures of the time.

All this suggests that the command to marry only a fellow believer is not timeless. However, we should also ask what the purpose of those original commands was. The warnings in the Old Testament imply a danger that intermarriage would result in pressure to change religion (Exod 34:16; Deut 7:3–4; 1 Kgs 11:3–4), and this was also the case in New Testament times. Does that apply today? Yes, though not in such a formal sense. It is no longer an expected requirement that couples should share the same religion, though their lives can certainly be easier and closer if they do. Now, as in New Testament times, there is likely to be friction between partners who do not share a love for Jesus. However, now as then, they may be won over by the genuine gentle witness of a Christian lifestyle (1 Pet 3:1).

One thing we can be certain of: God recognizes the validity of marriages between a believer and nonbeliever and loves both the children and the nonbelieving partner just as much as their believing parent and partner loves them.

14

▼

Wifely Submission

Rebellion against the patriarch was considered immoral in Roman society, so Christian wives and slaves were told to submit for the sake of the gospel. The situation has changed, so should Christian lifestyle change?

Men are traditionally supposed to be the brave and strong protectors of their wives. And yet, in the greatest physical danger faced by my wife during our marriage I wasn't able to help much at all. Her clenched teeth, groans, and occasional screams told me how serious it was, but there was nothing I could do except hold her hand and pray as she delivered our babies.

With modern medical care, death in childbirth is very low (about one in ten thousand),[1] though this is nearly four times higher than the likelihood of being killed in a car crash during the same year.[2] In the ancient world, about a third of women

---

1. For modern UK figures, see NHS, "Around 1 in 10 Maternal Deaths Due to Flu" (TinyURL.com/MaternalDeath).

2. In 2013 there were about 1,700 road deaths in the UK (see the table at TinyURL.com/RoadDeathUK), which has a population of about 65 million. This was a chance of 1 in 38,000 that a person would die in a road accident during that year.

died giving birth[3]—far more than the number of men who died in battle or while hunting. No wonder Genesis says that painful childbirth is one of two consequences that women suffered when Eve sinned. The other is submission to her husband (Gen 3:16). Men suffered painful labor of a different kind: weeds and poor soil turned farming into backbreaking toil (vv. 17–19).

We have been able to minimize three of these consequences of Adam and Eve's sin using analgesics, weed killer, and tractors—something we surely all thank God for. But what about wifely submission? Is this something that we should still encourage?

POWERFUL HELPER

Being a perfect Old Testament wife did not equal being weak. Eve is called Adam's "helper" (Gen 2:20; Hebrew *ezer*)—a word used elsewhere only of God and warriors who give protective "help." And the perfect wife in Proverbs 31 is a successful entrepreneur. She starts by selling homemade clothes to foreign merchants at the port (vv. 13, 14, 24), and with the profits she buys land and builds up a wine business (vv. 16–18). Consequently, her husband doesn't need a wage, so he works as a city magistrate (v. 23). She is also generous to the poor and finds time to manage her household servants and teach her children (vv. 15, 20, 26–28).

That description of a perfect wife was written by King Lemuel—not by King Solomon, who had a very different view of women (perhaps because he'd been married to so many!—1 Kgs 11:3). The proverbs attributed to Solomon include many warnings about women who are wicked, loud, or nagging—for

---

3. Before antibiotics, about 50 in 1,000 births resulted in the mother's death. See Geoffrey Chamberlain, "British Maternal Mortality in the 19th and Early 20th Centuries" (TinyURL.com/MaternalDeathUK). For an average of seven births per woman, this means one in three mothers died this way.

example, Proverbs 6:25–29, 11:22, and of course 27:15: "A quarrelsome wife is like the dripping of a leaky roof in a rainstorm." But I think this tells us more about the author than the gender.

Romans regarded the ideal woman as submissive, demure, and thrifty. But these ideals started to crumble just before New Testament times, when an emancipation movement started. This became a subject of debates in the Senate, and their speeches show how frightened Roman men were of this. Wives had recently gained the legal right to spend their own money without their husband's permission, and fortunes were disappearing on hairstyling and jewelry.[4] By New Testament times, women were also enacting equality by taking lovers just like their husbands did.

Josephus, a Jewish historian, took the opportunity to commend Judaism to his Roman readership through his comments about women. While married to his third wife, he wrote in *Against Apion* that Jewish Scripture says: "The woman is in all things inferior to the man."[5] This was a lie, of course—there is no text like that in the Bible—but he knew his readers would love it. He then summarized the law of Moses in a way that mirrored Roman household management.[6] This was based on Aristotle's three maxims: wives should submit to husbands, children should submit to fathers, and slaves should submit to masters.[7]

---

4. The *Lex Oppia*, c. 200 BC (TinyURL.com/WikiLexOppia), funded the war against Carthage by limiting what women could spend on luxury. Men tried to keep this law because, as Cato said, "As soon as the law no longer imposes a limit on your wife's extravagance, you certainly will not be able to impose it" (Livy, *History of Rome* 34:3.1–3, trans. Evan Sage [TinyURL.com/LivyRestraint]).

5. Josephus, *Against Apion* 2.25, trans. William Whiston (TinyURL.com/JosephusHousehold).

6. Josephus, *Against Apion* 2.25–31 (starting at TinyURL.com/Josephus Household).

7. "The science of household management has three divisions, one the relation of master to slave ... the paternal relation, and the third the conjugal, for

Paul and Peter also commended Aristotle's threefold submission, but for different reasons and with less enthusiasm. They agreed that slaves should submit, but added the caveat that masters should not misuse them. Likewise, they agreed that children should submit but added that fathers should not debase them. And they agreed that wives should submit but added that husbands should love them sacrificially (Eph 5:22–6:9; Col 3:18–4:1; 1 Tim 2:9–3:7; 6:1–2; 1 Pet 2:18–3:7).

It was important for Paul and Peter to commend Aristotle's rules (albeit with these caveats) because of the danger to the Christian message if they taught equality instead. They knew that encouraging a lack of submission in family life would be interpreted as immorality. If they taught equality, Christian wives would be regarded like the licentious Roman equal-rights women, so nonbelievers would "malign" their religion (Titus 2:5). They therefore told Christians to submit even to cruel masters and unbelieving husbands in order to advance the gospel (1 Pet 2:18–21; 3:1–2; 1 Tim 6:1).

I find it impressive and humbling that believers in New Testament times were willing to put up with cruel masters and micromanaging husbands so that people wouldn't get a bad impression about their new religion. If they hadn't done this, Christianity would have had a much harder time spreading.

In the Old Testament, things are surprisingly more lax. There is no command that women should submit—unless you include the one that caused all the trouble in Queen Esther's day. Her predecessor, Queen Vashti, was ordered "to display her beauty" to the king's party guests who had been drinking for the past

---

it is part of the household science to rule over the wife and children [as well as slaves]" (Aristotle, *Politics* 1.5.1 = 1259a, 37–40, trans. H. Rackham [TinyURL.com/AristotlePoliticsHousehold], and expounded in *Economics*).

seven days. When she refused, he dismissed her and made a new law that "all the women will respect their husbands ... so that every man should be ruler over his own household" (Esth 1:20–22). The book of Esther was written partly as a Jewish reaction against this kind of thinking, which was becoming the norm. The woman in Proverbs 31 suggests that Jewish women had overall responsibility over household matters, and a good marriage involved teamwork. However, women regarded their husband as the leader of that team, because the normal Hebrew word for a husband was *ba'al*, that is, "lord."

WITH MY BODY I THEE WORSHIP

Is the submission of wives a timeless command? There is certainly continuity between the Old Testament and the New. Wives were expected to submit to their husbands, and this worked well when mixed with mutual respect. However, this was certainly influenced by the culture of the times. The Old Testament didn't specifically teach this because it was already an ingrained aspect of ancient culture, and when it does mention the subject it appears to emphasize respect for women. Aristotle's rules were similarly widely accepted in New Testament times, and they appear to be cited only in order to add restrictions to them. After all, if husbands love their wives as sacrificially as Christ does, then submission is seen in a whole new light. So this rule is unlikely to be timeless because it always mirrors the prevailing cultures, and the Bible authors express concerns about aspects of it.

So should Christian wives submit to their husbands in today's culture? Well, that depends partly on what couples promise to do in their own marriage vows!

Traditional marriage vows reflect the language of Ephesians 5:21–29, where we are told that Christ loves, cherishes, and nourishes his church. Later, when these three became marriage vows, the language morphed into "love, honor, and keep." At some point, the word "obey" was added. Presumably this also derives from Ephesians 5—"wives submit." However, in Ephesians these words follow immediately after an injunction for both men and women to "submit to one another" (vv. 21–22). This indicates an ambivalence in the Christian world about submission, also found in the Jewish world. In some surviving Jewish marriage certificates, the bride promises to obey her new husband, and in a small number, the groom also says he will obey his wife.

The marriage service in the Anglican Book of Common Prayer (1662) remained almost unchanged from a much earlier English marriage service, the *Use of Sarum* (1085), which already included "love, honour and keep." In it the bride also promised "to be bonny and buxom in bed and at board." This vocabulary needs a little explanation: "bonny" used to mean "good," "buxom" meant "obedient," and "board" referred to mealtimes, as in the phrase "bed and board." So this meant "be good and obedient, night and day." Sadly, this was replaced by the more prosaic language "to obey."

But the old marriage service does not only demand submission from wives. Traditional grooms also promised to submit when they said: "With my body I thee worship." The old English "to worship" means "to serve obediently." It survives in Shakespeare, such as when Jack Cade says he will dress his servants in uniform livery so they can better "worship me, their lord."[8] And we still use it in court in England when we call the judge "your worship." This isn't because he is godlike, but because we acknowledge our submission to his court.

---

8. *Henry VI*, part 2, act 4, scene 2.

Surprisingly, the one-sided obedience by a wife is a very recent innovation in Church of England wedding vows. Until a few years ago, if a woman promised to obey in her vows, the man also had to promise "to worship" (that is, obey). This was reiterated as a fixed rule in the 1980 *Alternative Service Book*: if the bride chose to say "love, cherish, and *obey*," then the groom had to reply with "love, cherish, and *worship*." The first time that brides were allowed to promise to "obey" without her husband reciprocating it was in the year 2000, when *Common Worship* was published and didn't contain this rule.

So submission by the wife alone was not available in Church of England wedding vows before this millennium. Couples had to either omit "obey" or had to promise to submit to each other, as in Ephesians 5:21. I can't help thinking that this latter promise is better than the modern emphasis on individual rights and self-determination. Two people committed to serving each other are much more likely to live harmoniously than one or both of them trying to be the boss.

Section 4

▼

Church Issues

15

▾

Female Leaders

Paul concluded that females were uneducated and thereby too gullible to lead a church. His conclusion was sensible, and so was his proposed solution: to educate them. He'd be surprised that women are now well educated but are still often kept out of leadership.

I feel such an idiot that I was so easily misled, but I was only a teenager, so perhaps my age excused me. I had asked my minister why women weren't allowed any leadership roles in the church. He answered: "Because women have always been the main supporters of heretical movements. It isn't their fault, but they are more easily deceived by the devil." As examples he pointed to the prophetess Jezebel from Revelation and the women who split the church at Philippi (Rev 2:20; Phil 4:2). I accepted his explanation completely and didn't question it for many years. I didn't even consider how paradoxical it was that those who chose to come to his services (as in many other churches) included more women than men!

Women have always been the mainstay of religions, both dubious ones and established ones—even male-run religions like ancient Judaism. For example, the non-Jews who chose to attend synagogues in Roman times were mainly women.[1] We

---

1. Many of these converted to Christianity; see, e.g., Acts 14:1; 17:1–4.

know this from the many synagogue inscriptions that refer to these "Godfearers"—80 percent of their names are female.[2] But their support didn't help Judaism to gain acceptance in the eyes of Romans because Romans regarded women as easily duped.

GULLIBLE WOMEN

Jews had the same attitude, and first-century Jewish historian Josephus even blamed gullible women for the expulsion of Jews from Rome. He admits that the expulsion was due to a group of Jewish men who swindled money from a rich Roman under the guise of contributing to Jerusalem's Temple—but somehow he manages to push the blame onto the rich woman, Fulvia, whom they duped. He managed this partly by linking the account with another extraordinary deception of a gullible woman. Paulina, a chaste senator's wife, refused the advances of a Roman called Mundus. She was a pious devotee of the goddess Isis, so he hatched a scheme to "appear" to her as the god Anubis while she was in the temple of Isis alone at night. In this guise he was able to convince Paulina to sleep with him. Josephus managed to detract from the guilt of the Jewish men by implying that all women are too easily misled.[3]

Josephus' readers would have nodded their agreement— these stories confirmed what they already knew, that women are gullible and empty-headed. Elsewhere Josephus even "quotes" the Old Testament in support: "The woman is in all things inferior to the man."[4] Of course, this quote isn't anywhere in the

---

2. Shelley Matthews, *First Converts: Rich Pagan Women and the Rhetoric of Mission in Early Judaism and Christianity,* Contraversions: Jews and Other Differences (Stanford, CA: Stanford University Press, 2001), 67.

3. Josephus, *Antiquities* 18.3.4 (TinyURL.com/JosephusPaulina).

4. Josephus, *Against Apion* 2.25, trans. William Whiston (TinyURL.com/JosephusHousehold).

Bible, but the fact that Josephus *thought* it was shows how convinced he was of this principle.

At first reading, Paul's advice to Timothy about women shows that he is equally mistrusting. In 1 Timothy 2:11–15 he implies that women are more gullible by pointing out that Eve (not Adam) was deceived by the serpent and says women should therefore not teach or have authority over men. Actually (as we saw in chapter 7, "Should Girls Be Educated?"), Paul considered that Eve's deception was due mainly to poor education of women. Unlike other Jews and Romans, who excluded women from education, Paul was in favor of helping women to learn.

Paul's mistrust might also be inferred from the extraordinary word he used when he warned about women who "usurp authority" over men (1 Tim 2:12 KJV). Recent research has shown that this rare word (*authenteō*) was normally reserved for extreme situations of domination or manipulation, though in the centuries after the New Testament was written the meaning gradually changed to a gentler "have authority."[5] This means that earlier English translations (such as the Geneva Bible and KJV) got it about right when they translated it "usurp authority," whereas some modern ones translate with a gentler phrase such as "have authority."

UNTRUSTWORTHY WOMEN

It sounds unlikely that women could "usurp authority" or "exercise dominance" over men in a world where men ruled every aspect of life, but actually pious Jews *were* afraid of women in three key areas of life. These activities affected them every day,

---

5. A good summary can be found in A. C. Perriman, "What Eve Did, What Women Shouldn't Do: The Meaning of αυθεντεω in 1 Timothy 2:12," *Tyndale Bulletin* 44 (1993): 129–42 (TinyURL.com/Perriman-TB44-1).

every week, and every month. Every day women baked bread and made the "dough offering," every week they lit the Sabbath lamp on Friday night, and every month they became a source of menstrual uncleanness. These seem like minor matters to us, but in Jewish law these were very serious for any pious Jewish man who was married to a wife who was not trustworthy. If a dough offering was not separated out, then the household bread contained a holy portion that warranted death if eaten by a non-priest. If the lamp wasn't lit before the Sabbath started (it started on Friday evening, often while the men were still at synagogue), they'd have to eat their special Sabbath meal in pitch darkness. If his wife didn't warn him about her menstrual status, he would become ritually unclean merely by sitting on the same couch as her.

The rabbis mistrusted women, fearing that they'd forget about these important duties. So they put the fear of God into women—literally—by teaching them this saying: "Women die in childbirth for three reasons—because they are not meticulous in the laws of menstrual separation, of dough offering, and of kindling the Sabbath lamp."[6] That is, if wives neglected any of these three key duties, then God would punish them by letting them die in childbirth. Childbirth was the most common cause of death for young women, so this was a very potent and nasty threat.

Paul undermined this teaching by reversing the saying at the end of this chapter in Timothy. Instead of "Women will die in childbirth if ..." he says: "Women will be saved in childbirth if ..." And instead of listing three things the women must *do*, he

---

6. Mishnah *Shabbat* 2:6 (TinyURL.com/Shabbat2-6). The origin of this is very early because dough offerings became much less important after the Temple was destroyed in AD 70, though some pious households did still follow this rule.

lists what they should *be*—full of "faith, love and holiness." Paul portrayed God as one who cares, protects, and rejoices in a pure heart—not one who punishes minor infringements of ceremonial law. Women, for Paul, are faithful, trustworthy, and loved by God. They aren't the fearsome sources of contamination who are under threat of special punishment, as in ancient rabbinic Judaism.

Women were not the best people to lead the church in Paul's day. They lacked education, so the only way they could have a major influence was by manipulation or bullying—which are often resorted to by poor teachers. Paul didn't think they were incapable of teaching—after all, he said they should teach younger women about their household duties (Titus 2:3–4) because this was something they knew about, more than men did. What they couldn't do was teach men: "I do not permit a woman to teach or to assume authority over a man" (1 Tim 2:12).

WOMEN AND AUTHORITY TO TEACH

Is this a timeless command? We cannot know whether this command changed with time because nothing like this was needed in the Old Testament. However, we do know that this reflected the culture of Paul's time, and a culture-reflecting command is likely to be limited to that culture. One thing to note in this ruling is that teaching implied authority. Some interpreters have tried to separate the two halves of the sentence as if Paul meant "women shouldn't teach, and also, as an entirely separate issue, they shouldn't assume authority over men either." But Paul can't have meant this, because women *were* allowed to teach— they taught women. So the first half needs the word "men" from the second half to make sense, which means that "teaching" in the first half is also linked to "authority" in the second half. To teach men implied authority over them, which was totally contrary to the prevailing culture of the time.

Today's teachers are completely different. Teachers used to embody knowledge itself, and they conveyed it to their pupils in a form that they could memorize, so that they could quote their teacher. A teacher today is someone who collects information and conveys it in a way that promotes understanding and healthy skepticism about things that are uncertain. The teacher is not regarded as having an importance or authority that is superior to their pupils. In fact, any university student who does not question what their teacher says is considered to be inadequate or lazy.

When people bring up this verse I usually reply: I do not accept the authority of any woman's preaching, and also I do not accept the authority of any man's preaching—I will only accept preaching that is based on the authority of the Bible.

Today, both the church and society have listened to Paul's plea that women should be educated and trusted because "nor is there male and female, for you are all one in Christ Jesus" (Gal 3:28). Women do not yet hold the same number of high-ranking positions as men, but those who do are equally competent and respected—in almost all institutions, except the church. Many churches still follow Paul's solution for the iniquitous situation he was seeking to change. Paul concluded that the current lack of education for women made them incapable of leadership. He would rejoice today that the situation has changed and women are no longer mistrusted or uneducated. But he would be horrified to see that the church is still acting as though they are.

16

▾

Self-Promoting Leaders

Jesus and Paul severely criticized those who liked important titles and advertised their impressive achievements. This is uncomfortable in today's corporate life and in professionally written résumés.

When I began looking for my first job as a church leader, I thought I would find one easily—after all, I had a doctorate from Cambridge. Instead, I found it difficult to even get an invitation to preach. I think prospective churches assumed that I must be either too high-minded or heretical. In the end, I was called to a church that knew me before I had gained additional titles. Many more churches now positively look for a minister with a doctorate. A doctor of ministry qualification is especially popular, so an increasing number of church notice boards boast that their minister has a DMin. Some have called this the "DMin-ization" of the church (you have to say it out loud to get it) because it can represent the insidious sin of pride.

Jesus said that Christian leaders should not be called by any honorific title. He gave examples of titles he rejected—rabbi, father, instructor—and suggested instead that they should be "servants" (Matt 23:8–11). And he criticized those Pharisees who "love the place of honor at banquets and the most important seats in the synagogues" (Matt 23:6). Suddenly I feel guilty—I too love the few occasions when this happens. And churches generally do the opposite of what Jesus taught about pride.

FANCY TITLES

All three terms proscribed by Jesus are equivalent to ones we use commonly today. "Rabbi" means, literally, "my master," though later it came to mean "teacher"—it is an honorific title like "Sir" or "Reverend." The title "Father" was an even greater designation of respect in the days when elders and especially parents were given great deference. This form of showing respect is still in use by Catholic churches, and it carries respect in a similar way to "Elder," used in many other churches. The word Matthew used for "instructor" (*kathēgētēs*) was relatively rare and meant "teacher" or "guide to knowledge of the highest kind." It was the title given to Ctesibius, an inventor in the third century BC, whose water clock remained the most accurate clock ever built for eighteen hundred years; he taught Heron of Alexandria, who invented a steam engine a few decades before Jesus. So perhaps the best modern equivalent for this word is "Doctor" or "Professor."

Like the Pharisees, the Greeks and Romans wanted to trumpet their achievements and qualifications. When a teacher was setting himself up in a town, he hired a hall and invited everyone for a free oration. These were popular events, because sometimes they were truly fascinating and informative, and even if they weren't it was fun to watch the speaker being humiliated by an audience who made their feelings known loudly. A successful orator would be one who employed all the flourishes taught in rhetoric classes, was perfectly groomed, and confidently declaimed his superb qualifications.

Paul was the opposite—he wasn't much to look at, and he deliberately used plain speech instead of Greek rhetoric, without any boasting about his qualifications. He could have boasted that he learned under Gamaliel, who was one of the greatest Jewish teachers alive at the time. He could have dressed appropriately, in a formal toga—which he was qualified to wear as a Roman citizen—but we know that he didn't wear any marks of Roman citizenship (Acts 21:39; 22:25-28). Romans' dress would normally indicate their status—anything from freed slave to equestrian middle class or senator. Stripes on their clothes marked their rank as clearly as the pips on an army uniform, and jewelry indicated their wealth. But Paul spurned all this.

Actually, Paul had a problem: he probably wasn't very good at formal rhetorical speaking as taught in the Roman academies. This was similar to what we now call "inspirational speaking"— the skilled use of techniques for connecting with your audience, moving their emotions, and keeping their attention while you persuade them and make them believe that they always thought your way. Romans learned rhetoric as a major subject at school, and they would normally spend more time on this than mathematics or literature because they regarded it as far more useful in everyday life.

Many of the Corinthians rejected Paul's message because he was so unlike the popular orators of the time (1 Cor 2:1-3). He was a scholar and teacher, but he couldn't or wouldn't use rhetoric to help express himself in public. He explained to the Corinthians that this was a good thing, because it meant that they were converted by real facts authenticated by God's Spirit and not by worldly wisdom or persuasive inspirational speaking (1 Cor 2:4-5, 12-13). However, he didn't go so far as to condemn classical rhetorical speaking because Apollos (who had done a wonderful job in the church at Corinth) was a master of rhetoric. Paul gave praise where it was due—he had planted the seed, and Apollos had watered it. Unfortunately, many Corinthians saw things much more divisively; some preferred Paul's style, though many preferred Apollos.

Ignoring outward appearance and accomplishments is very difficult. We tell ourselves not to judge a book by its cover, but usually we do so anyway. It is hard to assess others dispassionately and almost impossible to assess yourself. Perhaps for most of us, Paul asked the almost impossible when he said: "Do not think of yourself more highly than you ought, but rather think of yourself with sober judgment" (Rom 12:3). But Paul wasn't merely trying to make people think of themselves as less important—he was also trying to get the humble to realize their own importance. He goes on to list various important people (prophets, teachers, leaders) mixed in with others whom he regarded as equally important: those who give encouragement, those who express mercy and forgiveness, those who love with sincerity, and those who give service, all with the brotherly affection of equals (Rom 12:4–10).

SERVANT HEART

Jesus gave an example no one could ignore, though they tried to. He didn't just act out the role of a servant—such as when he washed his disciples' feet—he regarded his servant role as essential for our salvation. The clearest statement we have from Jesus about how his life and death saves us is encapsulated in a single verse: "The Son of Man did not come to be served, but to serve, and to give his life as a ransom for many" (Matt 20:28 = Mark 10:45).

Jesus said, in effect, that it is not only his death that saves us but his life lived as a servant. His whole life, including his death, was given to serve others. And yet, as Paul pointed out, Jesus was the one person who would not be boasting if he made himself equal with God (Phil 2:6). The other two Gospels record this truth in different ways—John with the final foot washing, and Luke in a way that we could easily miss: he says that Jesus' ministry started when he was "about thirty" (Luke 3:23). The age of thirty would have made his readers think of two things: Levites start their full-time service at age thirty, and the minimum age at which a slave can be freed in Roman law is thirty. Therefore, in both cultures, this reminded them that Jesus was a servant, first as a manual worker to support his mother, and then in religious service for all of us. His whole life was given in service to others.

Jesus' rejection of honorific titles wasn't just for others; he called himself by the lowest title imaginable: "Son of Man." In Aramaic this was a phrase that meant "an ordinary man." If you wanted to say you met someone selling oranges, you'd say "I met a son of man selling oranges"—it just means "someone." Of course, it also reminds us of the phrase used in Daniel 7:13— the glorified "Son of Man"—but the whole point of using it in that passage was to indicate that an ordinary human was glorified by God. Jesus used this phrase to signify that he was fully human and in that sense "ordinary." But his followers always avoided using "Son of Man" when talking about Jesus on earth, because they thought this title was just too demeaning. Jesus also called himself a "shepherd," the lowest-ranking profession in Israel. When some rabbis debated whether stale or rotten food needed to be tithed, one rabbi suggested testing it by seeing whether a dog would eat it. But others said dogs eat everything, so they used the definition "if a shepherd will eat it."[1] They were at the bottom of society, and Jesus identified himself with them.

In the Old Testament, the model of humility was Moses. There is one verse in Numbers that must have been written by

---

1. Babylonian Talmud *Betzah* 21a (TinyURL.com/Betzah21A).

someone other than Moses, because it says: "Now Moses was a very humble man, more humble than anyone else on the face of the earth" (Num 12:3). This fits with what we know: Moses pleaded with God to let someone else lead, and in exasperation God let Aaron be his spokesman (Exod 4:10–14). He also refused God's offer to make a new nation from his offspring in place of sinful Israel, but instead spent forty days interceding for the nation (Exod 32:9–14; Deut 9:18–19). I don't think he was humble as a young man—being brought up as a prince in Pharaoh's palace isn't a great way to learn humility! I think God taught him during those years he spent doing the lowly work of a shepherd—culminating in that day he took his sheep up Mount Sinai (Exod 3:1–2).

Humility as a virtue is regarded as an antidote to the terrible vice of pride throughout the Bible, but the only practical command we have concerning this is Jesus' teaching on titles. We can't say that this is timeless by virtue of being constant through the Bible because there was little need for this command in the Old Testament. However, its timelessness is indicated by the fact that it was countercultural. Status was very important for Jews and Romans, so the idea of deliberately rejecting honorific titles was very strange indeed.

The early church took Jesus' teaching on this subject seriously. Although it inherited the titles "elder" and "priest" from the synagogue, when the church invented its own titles it chose "deacon" and "minister"—i.e., the Greek and Latin words for "servant." Even "apostle" merely meant "a messenger," someone who was only important if he carried an important message.

Today we are again in a society where we are expected to sell ourselves at every opportunity, from employment résumés to conversations at parties. Often we cunningly find self-effacing ways to communicate how qualified, skilled, or experienced we

are without appearing to boast. And if we don't have formal qualifications we boast about our fitness, possessions, prospects, or
relationships. Few people stand against the trend like Paul did.
Inspirational speaking is also highly regarded, and although
Paul didn't reject this, he did warn about its misuse because, too
often, it merely brings honor to the speaker.

In C. S. Lewis's vision of heaven in *The Great Divorce*, the nar-
rator meets the procession of a great lady in a fine chariot preceded by beautiful dancers and musicians. His guide explains
that she was Sarah Smith, who was a "nobody" on earth, and
all those who are enjoying heaven with her are the many souls
she saved by showing them love and the source of love. One day,
heaven will reveal the true value of our lives, and our boasting
will burst like bubbles.

17

▼

Conversion or Tolerance?

The Bible appears very intolerant of other religions, urging their fol-
lowers to convert. Actually, it only condemns dangerous and destruc-
tive aspects of other religions. Admittedly, Christians want everyone
to find Jesus.

Jews often joke that they don't want to convert you to Judaism: "You probably have enough problems already." Behind the humor is a serious point that makes me avoid converting Jews to the *religion* of Christianity. That is, I don't want them to adopt a new set of religious practices and institutional structures to replace ones they are used to. But I do want them to find Jesus and worship him as their Savior and Lord. It doesn't really matter whether they then join a traditional church or, like Messianic Jews, choose to continue most of their old Jewish observances. The important thing is that they know Jesus and trust him for forgiveness of sins.

Is this wishy-washy nonconfrontational tolerance? Actually, it's the same attitude that New Testament Christians had. They were zealously evangelistic and, at the same time, tolerant of other religious lifestyles among converts. So long as converts followed Jesus, it didn't matter whether they followed a Jewish lifestyle or not.

This tolerance wasn't due to cowardice. Paul preached Jesus at every opportunity, even while he was on trial or when facing a hostile mob (Acts 21:2–22:24; 25:23–26:32). Tolerance wasn't adopted for the sake of an easy life. If Christians had wanted to escape persecution, they could have pretended that being a Christian was simply a form of Judaism, and then the Romans couldn't have persecuted them because Julius Caesar had given Jews the right to practice their religion. By pointing out that practicing Judaism was not sufficient for salvation, they got themselves persecuted by Jews and Romans alike. Despite these problems, they continued to point out that while Christian beliefs were different, continuing Jewish practices didn't matter much.

RELATIONSHIP, NOT RITES

Christianity wasn't a new "religion" in the sense that it had a host of new rites, rituals, or ceremonial procedures. Christianity was something very different—neither a set of religious practices nor a set of philosophical beliefs but a relationship with God through Jesus, the risen Christ. Unlike most philosophies, Christianity transformed people's lives and morals. Unlike most religions, it didn't introduce a new set of religious practices. Early Christians had no ceremonies or festivals of their own— unless you counted the special way they ended their meals and their once-only cleansing ceremony (baptism), both of which were adapted from Judaism.

Christians were, of course, very concerned about spiritual realities and morality, so they utterly rejected idolatry and immorality, but they didn't ask converts to give up any religious customs that weren't sinful. So long as their customs didn't conflict with God's laws, the normal practice for new believers was to live out their faith within their own culture and worship via their old ways of "doing" religion. Christianity transformed their inner life and morals, leaving their Jewish culture intact.

Because the first Christians were Jews, their lifestyle already excluded idolatry and immorality. They continued to worship on a Sabbath, heard sermons, and ate kosher food. They even frequented the Temple—not only because it was a good venue (Acts 2:46; 3:1), but because they brought sacrifices. This sounds to us today as though their adherence to their newfound Savior was somewhat lacking, but Jesus himself assumed they would still bring Temple offerings (Matt 5:20, 23). They followed these old practices long after Jesus' death.

Paul, for example, even made Jewish vows, which included shaving your head and bringing an offering to the Temple (Acts 18:18; 21:23-26). He also circumcised his Greek convert Timothy for the pragmatic reason that this helped get him into places where he could evangelize (Acts 16:3). This later caused trouble because people thought this meant he taught circumcision as part of salvation—he denied this by pointing out that Titus (who was also a Greek convert of his) wasn't circumcised (Gal 2:3). The point was that these practices could be followed or not, because they weren't needed for salvation.

Even Gentile converts often didn't need to change their lifestyles. Many of them already frequented synagogues rather than the Roman temples and followed Jewish morals. Such Gentiles were referred to as "Godfearers," often translated as "God-fearing Gentiles" in Acts (13:16, 26), and several ancient inscriptions in synagogues refer to them. Many of them heard the gospel in the synagogue and became Christians.

Not surprisingly, some Jewish converts misunderstood and thought that Christianity was merely a form of Judaism. So when Gentiles wanted to become Christians, they told them to convert fully to Judaism first. But Paul rejected this very firmly.

He allowed anyone to follow Jewish religious customs, but he vehemently forbade anyone from *requiring* Jewish practices such as eating kosher food or being circumcised (Gal 2:3–14). Jesus, similarly, criticized Pharisees for persuading Gentiles to follow their religious practices (Matt 23:15).

Gentile Christians could still use the baths and libraries even though they were dedicated to various pagan deities. Rabbi Gamaliel pointed out that a statue in the baths wasn't the same as an idol in a temple. He said that he urinated in front of Aphrodite's statue (because it stood in the urinal), so he could hardly be accused of worshiping it![1]

Paul even allowed Gentiles to eat meat that *might* have been offered to a god, so long as they recognized that the god was nothing. However, some believers thought this was wrong, so he urged people in his churches not to do it if such believers were present (1 Cor 8:10). This implies that the tolerance was not a militant stance of people standing on their rights, but an attitude of harmony whenever possible. Paul's maxim was: "If it is possible, as far as it depends on you, live at peace with everyone" (Rom 12:18). If Paul had his way, there would be no interfaith violence or even antagonism.

At first glance, the Old Testament is completely intolerant. It bans special haircuts and tattoos simply because they were used by followers of certain cults (Lev 19:27–28). Kings are praised for destroying pagan altars (2 Kgs 23:1–25), and Elijah even murdered all the priests of Baal (1 Kgs 18:40). However the attitude of one's heart was more important than religious practice. For example, after Naaman decided to follow the God of Israel, he still had to accompany his king when he worshiped in Rimmon's temple.

---

1. Mishnah *Avodah Zarah* 3:4 (TinyURL.com/AvodahZarah3-4).

He asked what he should do, and Elisha said this was OK so long as Naaman didn't actually make any offerings (2 Kgs 5:17–19).

People with other religions were allowed to live inside Israel and had full protection of the law, just like those who practiced Judaism. A non-Jew who lived in Israel had equal protection under Israelite law: "The same law applies both to the native-born and to the foreigner residing among you" (Exod 12:49; Num 15:16, 29). They were encouraged to become Jews by circumcision because they could then join in with the festivals (Exod 12:48). But even if they remained in their own religion, their employer couldn't make them work on a Sabbath (Exod 20:10). Although they had these benefits, they weren't constrained by food laws (Deut 14:21). So in some ways they were better off than Jews, because they had all the protection of the law and none of its religious constraints.

NOT ALL TOLERANCE IS THE SAME

Some kinds of toleration are very different from that in the Bible. Roman society expected everyone to be tolerant of all religions by actually worshiping all the gods. When Romans conquered a land, they supported and embraced the religions practiced there. In Judea, for example, Emperor Augustus initiated an annual subscription to pay for sacrifices in the Jerusalem Temple. Romans made friends and business partners by eating meals in each other's temples, and a wife was required to add her husband's gods to those that her family worshiped.

Roman tolerance meant that everyone *had* to join in with worship; Christian tolerance meant that no one should be *forced* to do this. The Romans simply couldn't understand why Christians wouldn't even offer a drop of wine or say a few words of worship to the divine emperor. They misinterpreted Christians' stand against idolatry as disrespect for all gods, so they were condemned as atheists—a major crime in Rome.[2]

Another form of tolerance that is often advocated today is letting everyone believe whatever they want without trying to persuade them otherwise. This is certainly different from what we find in the New Testament, where Christians enthusiastically share the good news they have discovered even when people don't at first want to believe it. Paul evangelized continuously: "Every Sabbath he reasoned in the synagogue, trying to persuade Jews and Greeks" (Acts 18:4). Very often he continued long past his welcome and was thrown out (Acts 9:20–25; see also 13:42–50; 14:1–6; 17:1–5; 18:4–6; 19:8–9).

TOLERANCE—WITHIN LIMITS

All this means that tolerance with regard to different religions is a timeless command in the Bible. The Old Testament commands that non-Jews must have the same civil rights without being forced to follow Jewish customs, and the New Testament teaches that even Christians shouldn't be criticized for following the religious rites of a different religion. There is, of course, a line: both the Old and New Testament say that no offerings should be made to an idol. But Naaman was allowed to go into the temple of Rimmon, and Christians continued to worship in the Jewish Temple. This law is countercultural because most countries in the ancient world gave special status to those who followed their religion—as Daniel and his friends found out (Dan 3; 6). And Roman society *claimed* to be tolerant but was actually the opposite.

---

2. See William R. Schoedel, "Christian 'Atheism' and the Peace of the Roman Empire," *Church History* 42, no. 3 (September 1973): 309–19 (TinyURL.com/Schoedel-Atheism).

Unfortunately, Christianity soon became just as intolerant. In the fourth century, when Constantine gave Christianity legal status, it started to be corrupted by power. It lost its unique emphasis on a relationship with God through Jesus and became just like other religions, emphasizing rituals and rules.

Today most Christians have rediscovered the Bible's teaching on tolerance for practices from other religions. New converts are encouraged to worship Jesus within the culture they are used to. If people want to wear hoodies or short skirts to church, or worship in the function room of a pub, that's OK.

One interesting development is that some converts in Islamic or Hindu cultures, where conversion is illegal or sometimes dangerous, have decided to worship Jesus within the rites of their cultural religion. It will be interesting to see what such believers will do if their society eventually becomes tolerant enough for them to worship openly as Christians. Will they decide to keep praying to Jesus five times a day in Arabic, kneeling with foreheads to the ground, facing Jerusalem?

If they do, I hope they are welcomed, because this is very similar to what Messianic Jews do and what the first Christians converts did in Jerusalem. And Paul defended their rights to do so.

18

▼

Church Discipline

Because Paul told Christians to avoid Roman courts, many Christians have failed to report things such as abuse. Jesus showed the true role of church discipline was to help reform and prevent exclusion, not to deal with criminals.

Child abuse in churches has become such a terrible scandal not just because of the malicious harm done to children, but also because of the cover-ups. Church officials who didn't want these things to become public simply moved the perpetrators on to another parish where, sometimes, they repeated the offense. This failure to deal seriously with crime and prosecute the offenders created a continuing climate of mistrust.

This church practice was inspired by Paul's teaching that believers should not be taken to secular courts, because the church should be able to deal with such problems internally (1 Cor 6:1–7). Historically this has given rise to church courts, which still exist in Catholic, Anglican, and many other churches. They can no longer judge cases that come under the purview of secular courts, but they still hear cases of church discipline. They have dealt with all kinds of offenses, from playing games on Sunday to sexual misconduct by clergy. But do Paul's words mean we should not take believers to secular court and use church courts instead?

LUCRATIVE PROSECUTIONS

The Roman courts, which Paul didn't want believers to use, were very different from courts today. Prosecuting someone was profitable in Roman law because the fine (which could be half the estate of the guilty person) went mostly to the successful prosecutor. This meant that the state didn't need to bring prosecutions, because private citizens could be relied on to prosecute each other for profit. But the high stakes made bribery commonplace, and the system soon became corrupt. Courts became the sporting ground where the rich fought using oratory and money against their enemies and anyone else whom they wished to humiliate. As James said about the rich: "Are they not the ones who are dragging you into court?" (Jas 2:6).

One way out was to use private arbitration, which was allowed in Roman law if both parties agreed. So Paul said that the church should itself arbitrate internal disputes and misconduct. Crimes such as murder or treason would still have been dealt with by the Roman courts, but cases of immorality or refusal to pay debts could be dealt with internally.

However, even in countries where secular courts are open and fair, churches have continued to hide their scandals by using their own discipline procedures. Child-abuse cases are just the tip of the iceberg. In private hearings of church courts today, ministers can be removed from their posts on grounds that would be dismissed by any employment tribunal. At the same time, other ministers can be privately "disciplined" for serious offenses with no more punishment than a caution and removal to a new parish.

For Paul, the scandal lay in the way that Christians took each other to court for profit. Today, the scandal lies in the way the church tries to hide that a member of the clergy has committed an immoral and/or criminal act. Their motive is to prevent the church being tarnished by these crimes, so they say things like: "He's just one bad apple." However, the last thing you do with a real bad apple is put it back in with the good apples.

A church can also move to the opposite extreme and excommunicate all sinners in an effort to "purify" itself. At times in the past, and sometimes today, churches expelled members for minor moral offenses or small differences in doctrine. This too could be blamed on Scripture, because Jesus taught about how to excommunicate believers in Matthew 18:15–17: "If your brother or sister sins, go and point out their fault, just between the two of you. *If they listen to you, you have won them over.* But *if they will not listen,* take one or two others along, so that 'every matter may be established by the testimony of two or three witnesses' [Deut 19:15]. *If they still refuse to listen,* tell it to the church; and *if they refuse to listen even to the church,* treat them as you would a pagan or a tax collector."

The italicized repetitions tell us Jesus' emphasis. For Jesus, every stage was hopefully the one at which the offender would listen and return in repentance. If he listened to a private rebuke, the matter could stop there; if he listened to an official rebuke from two or three, then others need know nothing about it; and finally the whole church shared the task of helping him to change his ways. Only if all this failed did he "become like a Gentile and tax collector."

PROVIDE A WAY BACK

At this point, we have to consider how Jesus treated "Gentiles and tax collectors." Most Jews avoided them, but Jesus ate with them and spoke to them about the kingdom of God. Anyone who was expelled into this group became part of Jesus' parish. He wouldn't give up on them.

Paul was equally concerned about those who had been disciplined by the church. Although Paul insisted that those who
lived immoral lives should be expelled from the fellowship, he
was also concerned that they should be helped to return. When
Paul discovered that a member of the Corinthian church was
sleeping with his stepmother, he insisted that the church should
"hand this man over to Satan" and "Do not even eat with such
people" (1 Cor 5:1–5, 11).

This kind of excommunication was even more serious than
it sounds because he was to be thrown out of his association. In
Roman society, associations (also known as fellowship groups)
were extremely important, because they provided social welfare
for a member who lost their job or had an unexpected bereave-
ment. They met regularly, usually eating a meal together in a
temple and renewing their pledge of support for each other.
When people became Christians, they had immediate problems
with the religious elements of these meetings. So they left their
associations—just as Christians may leave secret societies, from
the Freemasons to Skull and Bones, for similar reasons. Christians
had to form their own Christian fellowship groups to replace the
security that their old group had provided. So, when this immoral
man was thrown out of the Christian fellowship group, he was
bereft—there was no state social security net, and he was on
his own.

Paul was concerned for him, and in his next letter to Corinth
Paul said he was horrified that the church was doing nothing to
try to rehabilitate him. "Now instead, you ought to forgive and
comfort him, so that he will not be overwhelmed by excessive
sorrow … in order that Satan might not outwit us" (2 Cor 2:6, 11).

Some churches make this same mistake because they interpret "do not associate or eat with him" to mean that they shouldn't

even speak to him. Paul's original readers understood what Paul meant: that he shouldn't be a member of their association and so he shouldn't share in their special meals. The nearest equivalent discipline that we can apply today is exclusion from Communion. This is the meal that represents membership of the church, and this is a fairly public means of showing disapproval.

The Old Testament contains no concept of religious courts or excommunication, because the state and religion were so closely connected, and courts were not really established. If someone had a dispute, they took it up with local leaders, who met "in the gate"—a literal reference to the large shaded area within the structure of a city gate. Here the case would be heard by elders (Deut 22:15; Prov 31:23) or perhaps even by the king (2 Sam 19:8), and people hoped to find vindication and justice there (Ps 127:5; Isa 29:21; Amos 5:10, 12, 15). The original elders were deputies of Moses (Exod 18:15–23) and specifically received the Holy Spirit to do this task (Num 11:16–17, 24–25), so it clearly wasn't regarded as a merely secular task.

There was a kind of excommunication in the Old Testament, but we have no idea how it worked. There were many offenses that were punished by being "cut off from the people." This was the punishment of someone who used holy anointing oil or incense simply to smell nice (Exod 30:33, 38) or ate a holy offering or blood (Lev 7:20–25; 17:27), or failed to keep the Passover (Num 9:13), or didn't repent on the Day of Atonement (Lev 23:29). These are all private sins, which they'd be likely to get away with—after all, who can tell if you have actually repented of your sins except God? So, instead of a court case ending in exile, they simply waited for God to act. If someone died before the age of fifty, it was generally assumed that God had "cut them off from the people"[1]—i.e., the Israelites left God to judge and punish these crimes.

RESCUE, NOT REJECTION

It is difficult to decide if excommunication is a timeless practice. It is certainly found in both Testaments, but it is significantly different. In the New Testament, the church was actively encouraged to be involved, mainly in order to try and help the individual repent. But in the Old Testament there was no procedure for people to judge, even though the first elders were filled with the Holy Spirit.

Are religious courts a timeless institution? Again, both Testaments had them, but they were very different. In the Old Testament they *were* secular courts—so they didn't act instead of them. And in the New Testament, Paul was using a provision of the secular law (allowing for arbitration) to let the churches avoid the corruption that was so easy in Roman law cases. And other organizations or families did the same thing. That is, his solution was reflecting the culture of his day.

The purpose of these laws in the Old and New Testament was fair and affordable justice. The legal situation today is very different. Most countries now have an open and fair judiciary, and avoiding it will only create suspicion or even scandal—as it has done. But justice is often not affordable, and arbitration is probably the best way to avoid high legal costs. Thanks to Paul's guidelines, the church is at the forefront of providing low-cost expert arbitration with organizations such as RESOLVE,[2] but these do not (indeed cannot) be used to avoid criminal cases being heard.

---

1. Babylonian Talmud *Moed Qatan* 28a (TinyURL.com/bMQ28a).
2. ResolveChristianMediation.com.

However, Jesus and Paul were more concerned with what happens before and after discipline is applied. Whatever the means by which a church dissociates itself from the immorality of members, this should always be preceded and followed by pastoral care. Jesus emphasized that every stage should be designed to help a sinner repent and remain inside the fold. And Paul emphasized that after excluding someone, there should be an all-out effort to bring them back.

The church exists for reforming sinners and shouldn't aim for perfect purity before Jesus returns. Church discipline is sometimes necessary, but the aim should still be that of rescue rather than rejection. As Rambo said: Leave no man behind!

Section 5

▼

Personal Vices

19

▾

Racism

Moses was almost deposed by a race riot when he married a black woman. Jesus' only recorded sermon concerned racism. The church listened, and the first Gentile convert was black. This is an issue the Bible doesn't hide.

My mother was an assistant in a stationery shop in Hamburg during Nazi rule. In 1938, the shop owner dismissed her and sent her to a shop owned by a friend. She was hurt, but he said it was for her own good. He was right; he was a Jew, and a few nights later came *Kristallnacht* ("Crystal Night")—a pretty name for an ugly event. Thugs roused by Hitler's anti-Semitic speeches smashed the windows of properties owned by Jews, looted their shops, and burned down synagogues. Over thirty thousand Jewish men were soon imprisoned in concentration camps, and this night started the movement that ended in six million deaths. The existence of pro-Nazi movements today reminds us that such racism hides just under the surface of many societies.

All nations are prone to xenophobia, and Jews themselves have not been immune. The Old Testament writers sometimes stressed the purity of Judaism, especially when the Israelites returned from exile in Babylon. As they were needing to reassert their national identity, Nehemiah told them to separate from all "foreigners" (Hebrew *erev*—Neh 13:3). However, this same word was also used to describe the large number of non-Israelites who were welcome to join them when leaving Egypt (Exod 12:38—where it is often translated as "mixed" or "other"). They not only marched across the Red Sea with the Israelites, but presumably married into the tribes that formed a new nation in Palestine. So although the Israelites regarded themselves as descended from one family of twelve brothers, their ancestors actually included people from other nations.

When the nation had been established, foreigners continued to join them—sometimes to simply visit, and sometimes to stay. Foreigners didn't have the right to own land, though they could buy a leasehold till the next Jubilee—an event that came every fifty years, when all land was returned to the family it had been originally allotted to (though we don't know whether this was often carried out in practice). Even so, many foreigners chose to stay because they didn't face discrimination. This was thanks to a clear command protecting foreigners: "When a foreigner resides among you in your land, do not mistreat them. The foreigner residing among you must be treated as your native-born. Love them as yourself, for you were foreigners in Egypt. I am the LORD your God" (Lev 19:34).

AS WHITE AS SNOW

However, color was a huge unspoken issue in early Israel. There was no problem when Moses married a Midianite, even though she was a foreigner (Exod 2:16–22). But when Moses married a black woman from Cush (modern-day Ethiopia/Sudan), a lot of people wanted to depose him from leadership, and his sister Miriam led a rebellion against him. God punished her in a frightening and dramatic way that highlighted her racism: he covered her completely with leprosy so that she was "as white as snow" (Num 12:10).

They probably picked up this racist attitude while living in Egypt. The lighter-skinned Egyptians looked down on the black Cushites. We see their attitude from the oath regularly sworn by witnesses in ancient Egyptian courts, saying that if they lied, "May my nose and ears be cut off, and may I be banished to the land of Cush."[1] They also looked down on any foreigners and couldn't bring themselves to eat with them. Even when Joseph invited his brothers to stay for a meal, he and his Egyptian friends ate apart "because Egyptians could not eat with Hebrews, for that is detestable to Egyptians" (Gen 43:32). Racism wasn't a problem just in Israel—it was everywhere.

Jesus' first sermon was on the subject of racism—and the people who heard it were so outraged that they tried to kill him. They dragged Jesus to a cliff top and tried to push him over, presumably in order to stone him (Luke 4:29). He'd angered them by pointing out that God healed the Gentile leper Naaman and sent Elisha to look after a Gentile widow during a famine. This implied that the many Jewish lepers and widows who were not helped lacked the faith shown by these Gentiles (vv. 25–27). This was a particularly sensitive issue for Jews at the time because they were fighting for their national identity in the face of the Roman invasion.

When Rome took over the governance of Palestine shortly before Jesus was born, their culture was far more disruptive than their army. Their gymnasium in Jerusalem offered the best education in the country, including unsurpassed facilities for sports, but these were carried out in the nude, which offended Jewish standards of decency. Elite households started copying

---

1. Alexandre Alexandrovich Loktionov, "May My Nose and Ears Be Cut Off: Practical and 'Supra-Practical' Aspects of Mutilation in the Egyptian New Kingdom," *Journal of the Economic and Social History of the Orient* 60 (2017): 263–91 (TinyURL.com/KushCurse).

Roman dining customs, lying on couches (which Jews normally did only at Passover) while being entertained by lady "sinners" (as the Gospels euphemistically call them). To stop their nation falling into these pagan ways, the Jews reacted jingoistically, teaching that all Gentiles were hated by God.

When Jesus criticized this xenophobia, it must have seemed as though he was siding with the enemy, but he continued to challenge it. Jews of his day were especially suspicious about Samaritans, whom they regarded as permanently ritually unclean. They had a saying: "Eating a Samaritan loaf is like eating the flesh of a pig."[2] Jesus' parable of the good Samaritan and his chat with a Samaritan woman at the well show that he didn't share these prejudices.

Jews living outside Palestine were not so racially intolerant. They knew there were good Gentiles because an increasing number of them even attended synagogues. The Jews called these Gentiles "Godfearers," and many synagogue inscriptions referring to them have been discovered in modern-day Turkey. This movement helps explain the enthusiastic welcome for the gospel in that area. However, the Jews weren't happy when Gentiles started becoming Christians and were accepted as equal members of this new faith. For example, Jews in Pisidia were happy to listen to Paul, but when Gentiles joined the crowd, they plotted against him (Acts 13:43–45).

COLOR-BLIND

The early church included black members, though it may be significant that we only hear about it incidentally. In fact, the first Gentile convert was black—a government minister from Ethiopia (Acts 8:27). We also know of Simeon Niger (i.e., "the

---

2. Mishnah *Shebiith* 8:10 (TinyURL.com/mShebi-8-10).

Black"), a leader of the church of Antioch (Acts 13:1). He wasn't called this to emphasize his color but because Simon/Simeon was an extremely common name, so Jews normally accompanied it with a second name. The Simon who helped Jesus carry his cross may also have been black because he was from Cyrene (modern-day Libya), though he may have been one of the many Jews who lived there. Mark recorded the names of his sons in his Gospel, as if his readers would recognize them (15:21), so probably the family became Christians and were well known to his readers. The interesting point in all of this is that no one bothered to mention the color of any of these people—it simply wasn't an issue in the early church.

The command against racial discrimination must be regarded as timeless because it is found in both Old and New Testaments, and it is countercultural in both. Most ancient societies were like Egypt—they considered themselves better than others and actively discriminated against foreigners. But Israel had a law specifically forbidding legal discrimination and telling Israelites to "love [foreigners] as yourself" (Lev 19:34).

When Jesus was asked, "Who is my neighbor?" (Luke 10:29), he used the parable of the good Samaritan to remind his audience of the command, even though his sermon against racism in his hometown had been received so poorly. The church succeeded where Israel failed: we have to dig between the lines to spot black people in the early church, because early Christians appear to have been color-blind. There were all kinds of races in the early church, and this was so normal that they hardly noticed.

Racism, ethnic conflict, and other forms of xenophobia are present in all societies today, as then—including, unfortunately, in many churches. It is difficult to comprehend how some church leaders encouraged the 1994 Rwandan massacre, or how

Afrikaner churches in South Africa used to preach the superiority of white races. Secular politicians have argued that Turkey could not join the European Union because it is not "Christian"—which is ironic because Turkey had churches before Europe did. But we mustn't be too quick to blame others without examining our own attitudes. Most of us subconsciously look down on those in society who have different lifestyles, dress codes, or attitudes from ourselves.

The church in the US is still struggling with the issue of racism, and in the UK secular society is often more integrated than churches. Blacks and whites tend to meet in separate congregations, and there are churches for specific nationalities such as Chinese. I've watched struggling Welsh-heritage Baptist churches in the valleys north of Cardiff (where I used to live) close down rather than join with nearby English Baptist congregations, even though very few of the Welsh members could actually speak Welsh! And when English Christians live abroad, they often attend expatriate congregations even if they have learned the local language.

The uproar that ensued when Moses married a black woman is a powerful story, especially when God punished the racism in such a visually appropriate way. It occurred to me that I've never heard a sermon on this, so I searched the huge database at SermonCentral.com. Among the two hundred thousand sermons uploaded there, I found thirty-eight on Numbers 12—which is impressive!—but only one of these mentions racism in this chapter. It seems that the church isn't very interested in this problem ... or maybe it's something we aren't willing to tackle yet.

20

▾

Alcohol and Other Drugs

Drink is common in the Bible, but it only condemns drunks. What about those who can't cope with moderation? And what about other drugs? The Bible has some clear guidelines.

The first funeral I did as a minister was of a man in his early twenties who didn't go to church—actually, he didn't really go anywhere: not to college, to work, or even out with friends. But one night some "mates" did manage to drag him out for a drink. He didn't understand alcohol, and they encouraged him to drink almost a bottle of brandy as if it were fruit juice. Then they helped him home, where he slept so deeply that he didn't wake up when he was sick. He inhaled his vomit and died.

Taken in moderation, alcohol does have some benefits. As a relaxant, it lowers blood pressure and reduces the inhibitions that stop some people from enjoying themselves. But statistically, alcohol is the most dangerous drug because it kills twice as many people as all illegal drug use totaled together, through accidents, illnesses, or alcohol-related violence.[1] So is alcohol

---

1. In the US, deaths from alcohol average 88,000 a year, compared to 21,382 deaths from drug misuse (excluding the 42,249 deaths from legal opioid prescriptions). See "Alcohol and Public Health: Alcohol-Related Disease Impact (ARDI)" (TinyURL.com/AlcoholDeathUSA and TinyURL.com/DrugDeathUSA for 2016). In the UK, the numbers are 7,327 for alcohol and 4,450 for all other drug misuse—see "Statistical Bulletin: Alcohol-Specific Deaths in the UK:

OK for Christians? After all, it is legal in most countries, and the Bible says it "gladdens human hearts" (Ps 104:15).

The Bible certainly has warnings about alcohol and condemnations of drunkenness, from Noah (who got drunk in Gen 9) to those who drink wine with the great harlot in Revelation 18. Proverbs associates alcohol with brawling, bruises, and mental confusion (Prov 21:1; 23:29–35). Paul condemns drunks alongside the sexually immoral, thieves, and slanderers, and says such people are outside the kingdom of God (Rom 13:13; 1 Cor 5:11; 6:9–10; Gal 5:21; Eph 5:18). However, although wine and beer can be severely misused by getting drunk, there is no hint that it was ever outlawed.

Two types of people *were* banned from drinking alcohol in the Old Testament: on-duty priests and Nazirites. Jews who took a long-term vow (called a Nazirite vow) were forbidden from drinking alcohol or cutting their hair (Num 6). Neither of these practices made them holy, but they were constant reminders to themselves and others about their vow to God. And priests who served at the altar were supposed to stay sober because making a mistake was potentially fatal (Lev 10:9). This was equivalent to the rule that you don't drink while operating dangerous equipment.

ADDICTIVE DRUGS

If the Bible allows alcohol, does that make other addictive substances OK—such as tobacco, heroin, and the bewildering number of other drugs on offer today? There are uppers such as ginseng, cocaine, amphetamines, etc., or emotive drugs such as alcohol, marijuana, skunk, heroin, MDA derivatives (the "love" drugs), and more. As a regular user, I feel the necessity

Registered in 2016" (TinyURL.com/AlcoholDeathUK) and "Statistical Bulletin: Deaths Related to Drug Poisoning in England and Wales: 2016 Registrations" (TinyURL.com/DrugDeathUK).

to speak up for my favorite drug: caffeine and the related xanthines found in tea, coffee, and chocolate. Five cups of tea or cans of Coke have about the same caffeine as a typical cup of coffee or a one-hundred-gram bar of dark chocolate.

How do we decide which ones are allowed? The simplest rule is that followed by Mormons: no nonmedical drugs are permissible, including alcohol, tea, and coffee. But reaching this conclusion requires creative Bible interpretation. Mormons claim that wine in Jesus' day was acceptable because it had a minimal alcohol content and was the only safe form of drink. However, wine in Jesus' day *did* make people drunk (e.g., Acts 2:13), and clean water *was* available in Jerusalem and elsewhere from natural springs and rivers. For example, the Pool of Siloam was fed with fresh water that was considered clean enough for Temple use,[2] and if you were too lazy, water sellers wandered the city carrying large skins with a tap.

Jesus certainly did drink alcohol. In his first miracle in John's Gospel he made water into wine, and we know it wasn't merely fruit juice because the master of the banquet declared it the "best" wine of the day (John 2:1-10). Some argue that this specially created wine could be wonderful without being alcoholic so Jesus and his disciples didn't have to drink alcohol. Perhaps, but at Passover it was impossible to escape alcohol. One of the requirements for celebrating Passover was drinking wine. If a poor person couldn't afford the necessary wine, he could get money from the local synagogue beggars' relief fund. In fact, the rabbis said that they *had* to ask for this money, even if they felt ashamed, because it was compulsory to drink wine at Passover.[3]

---

2. Mishnah *Sukkah* 4:9 (TinyURL.com/mSukkah-4-9).

3. Mishnah *Pesahim* 10:1 (TinyURL.com/mPesahim-10-1); Jerusalem Talmud *Pesahim* 10:1, 69a (TinyURL.com/yPesahim-10-1).

There are clear warnings in the Bible against getting drunk, as blunt as "Do not get drunk" (Eph 5:18). This is a timeless command, because we see the same warnings in the Old and New Testaments. And it is countercultural because alcohol abuse was common in cultures surrounding ancient Israel and especially in the Roman culture that Paul's followers came out of. This is therefore a command that God wants all his followers to obey, whatever kind of culture they live in.

Some Christians reject alcohol completely. Most Indian and African Christians do this because their translations of the Bible say that Jesus drank nothing but "grape juice." Some English denominations, such as the Salvation Army and Methodists, take a similar stance because they were founded at a time when alcohol was ruining society and Christians had to take a firm stand against it. Many independent churches use nonalcoholic wine for Communion for the similarly pragmatic reason that ex-alcoholics will not be excluded. Some even say that when Paul told Timothy to use wine for his stomach problems (1 Tim 5:23), he meant him to rub it in!

What about alcohol use without getting drunk? One might say it would have been better if the Bible had banned alcohol completely but, as so often, God asks us to do something more difficult: to be responsible and self-controlled. C. S. Lewis's fictional demon Screwtape points out that the devil never succeeded in creating anything evil, but has managed to corrupt many good things. Alcohol is a good example of this—a wonderful part of creation that has become the most dangerous recreational drug.

Of course, the Bible doesn't give any commands about evils that were unknown in the past, such as designer drugs, online pornography, or all-you-can-eat junk food. Similarly, it says nothing about the technology of distilling alcohol to make much stronger drinks, and no one in Bible times could have imagined that alcoholic drinks would be cheaper to buy than water, as they currently are in many supermarkets. Clearly, we need to look for principles in the Bible rather than specific commands, but what are they?

CLEANING OUR TEMPLE

Peter and Paul give us some clear motivations for avoiding drug misuse: "Your bodies are temples of the Holy Spirit. ... You are not your own; you were bought at a price" (1 Cor 6:19-20). And "you also, like living stones are being built into a spiritual house to be a holy priesthood" (1 Pet 2:5). This coheres well with the modern concepts of "cleansing" your body of drugs and keeping yourself "clean." The Corinthians had been influenced by the Stoic philosophy that you could do what you wanted with your body because it doesn't matter and won't last. They quoted sayings such as: "Food is for the stomach and the stomach for food, and God will destroy them both" (1 Cor 6:13), and "I have the right to do anything," which Paul countered with warnings that their bodies belong to the Lord and that they shouldn't "be mastered by anything" (1 Cor 6:12).

This gives us two Bible principles: we shouldn't take anything that harms us or that "masters" us. First, we should not take any drug that will cause us harm—either legal or illegal. Of course, we then have to consider which drugs are harmless in limited doses. We know that tobacco is addictive and harmful in any quantity, and drunkenness causes many deaths. But what about low amounts of alcohol, marijuana, or coffee? Should you take any amount of something that is a poison? It is true that caffeine can kill you if you ingest more than ten grams in one day. However, you'd need to drink one hundred mugs of coffee to get this dose, and the water in the coffee will kill you first because you will die of cerebral edema after drinking fifty mugs of water.[4] The point is that too much of anything can harm you.

The second principle is perhaps the most decisive: a drug is our master if it changes our behavior. This doesn't just include mind-altering drugs such as heroin or temporary boosters such as cocaine. Alcohol lowers our inhibitions so that we commit acts we would avoid when sober—anything from karaoke to adultery. We might even consider that caffeine changes our behavior because it tells our body to be awake when it wants to sleep—though whether this is harmful depends on how much sleep we lose. Christians consider themselves to be bought by Jesus and their bodies to be a temple for the Holy Spirit. So if they cause damage by drugs, or fall into sin because of drugs, this is a crime of both theft and sacrilege.

We should therefore ask these two questions about everything we use and potentially abuse: Does it harm us, and does it change our behavior? It is up to each of us to decide where that line should be drawn. However, looking at our society and medical statistics makes me wonder whether the church needs to give a clearer warning about drunkenness. Methodism was born at a time when society was suffering from gross alcohol abuse and decided to make a dramatic public stand against it. Personally, I make a half-hearted stand: whenever I'm at an event where I can't see nonalcoholic drinks, I specifically request one. But perhaps it is time to campaign and complain more loudly, for the sake of our society.

---

4. Coco Ballantyne, "Strange but True: Drinking Too Much Water Can Kill," *Scientific American*, June 21, 2007 (TinyURL.com/WaterCanKill).

21

▾

Is Gluttony a Sin?

In the Old Testament they killed gluttons, and in the church it became a "mortal sin." So why doesn't the New Testament take it so seriously, and why don't we?

The world now contains more people who are obese than malnourished. This change first happened a few decades ago, but then conflicts in areas such as Yemen and Congo caused local famines. However, obesity has continued to rise and has overtaken malnutrition again. This reminds us that the planet has enough food, and its lack is usually caused by human sin.

We wouldn't be in this happy condition without the invention of agriculture. It must have been an amazing genius who worked out that deliberately burying grain would actually produce more of it in a few months' time. Rice farming would have been even more difficult, because it requires flat fields with borders to allow periodic flooding.

Both types of agriculture worked best within large, organized communities. People have to specialize in different tasks—some do farming (which is a full-time job), while others defend them, or produce tools and other things that farmers need. The community needs to store the food because harvests come only once or twice a year, and in bad years they may need to organize rationing.

But what happens when someone in the community rebels? What if they get drunk and smash things up, or break into the stores and gobble up all the best food? Before the invention of iron locks and sticky mortar to hold stones together, breaking out of a building wasn't hard, so it was difficult to imprison a miscreant. In some rural Mongolian villages of circular yurts built from thick felt, they still tie a drunkard to a post until he sobers up because none of their buildings are secure. But the persistent actions of an antisocial individual could gradually drive a community into famine.

The Old Testament had a clear though severe solution: death. This type of person could cause the death of a community, and they couldn't incarcerate him for any length of time, so there was little choice. Banishment would be equivalent to moving a child molester in a church to another parish—it would merely antagonize neighboring communities. So the elders made a decision, and the whole community showed their agreement by helping to stone him. The heart-wrenching aspect of this law is the start of the process: the ones who had to bring him before the elders were his parents. They had to admit that they couldn't control their son and (no doubt tearfully) had to admit they had no other recourse. His actions were too dangerous to ignore.

In the New Testament, this law still remained in force, but no one applied it. Jesus was accused of being a glutton and drunkard by his enemies (Matt 11:19 = Luke 7:34), but they didn't attempt to arrest him for this because it no longer warranted the death penalty. They couldn't repeal a law given by God, but it appears that they could neglect to enforce it. Similarly, there is still a law against singing profane or obscene songs in Metropolitan London streets, but no one enforces it.[1]

---

1. "Legal Curiosities: Fact or Fable?" (TinyURL.com/LegalOddities).

Surprisingly, greed and gluttony resurface in the New Testament Letters as a very serious sin listed alongside sexual immorality and idolatry. The people who practice it are so terrible that Christians should not entertain them as guests (1 Cor 5:10–11); and these people should not expect to enter heaven (1 Cor 6:10; Eph 5:5). The actual word "gluttony" isn't used in most English New Testament translations, except rarely at 1 Peter 4:3, when translating *komos*, which the NIV and ESV translate as "orgies." This helps to remind us about what was actually happening in the Roman world.

ROMAN ORGIES

Romans really knew how to overindulge in all kinds of ways. If you think that modern bookshops and TV are fixated on food, you should sample ancient Latin literature. Although they still loved descriptions of battles like the Greeks did, there was a growing and voracious appetite for descriptions of banquets, with details of every course and delicacy. Middle and upper-class Romans spent a large proportion of their day eating or planning to eat. Lavish meals, often with entertainment, were the chief form of leisure and could last for hours. Meals bonded together business partners, political connections, friends, and family. A large part of a woman's role was organizing meals, and only unsociable men would neglect to give regular invitations to friends.

When the host was trying to impress, the courses could be endless. It was rude to refuse, so Romans perfected the art of making themselves vomit. This probably wasn't a regular practice, but at important banquets it could prove necessary. Otherwise guests would simply loosen their togas a little more. Overeating wasn't looked down on, but failing to appreciate a host's generosity could scratch one off his future guest list. So you kept eating and tried not to vomit in public.

Along with food came copious drink. Wives weren't invited to traditional banquets, so that the host could provide hired women for after-meal "exercise." When Paul and Peter referred to this type of meal (called a *komos*), they accurately associated them with sexual immorality and drunkenness (see Rom 13:13; Gal 5:21; 1 Pet 4:3).

So the "gluttony" translated from *komos* refers to something much worse than overeating. And the "greed" that Paul referred to in other passages (1 Cor 5:10–11; 6:10; Eph 5:5) translates *pleonektes*—which is "avariciousness" or "grasping," usually seeking money and power rather than food. This doesn't refer to overeating either, so where does the sin of gluttony come from?

DEADLY SIN

Gluttony didn't become a severe sin until the writings of the church fathers in the first few centuries after the New Testament. They promoted it to a "mortal" or "deadly" sin—by which they meant one that caused you to lose your salvation. Of course, only severe gluttony was "mortal": Aquinas defined this as the type of gluttony that causes you to break other laws of God in order to consume more.[2] And he warned that this includes more than just gluttony for food, but also for alcohol, and no doubt today he'd include drugs. However, lesser overconsumption was still regarded as a sin of gluttony, so that Augustine felt the need to confess to God that he sometimes ate till he was "full."[3]

Are commands against gluttony timeless, so that they apply to us today? The Old Testament law reflected the needs of the

2. See Aquinas's complete response at TinyURL.com/GluttonyAquinas.

3. "Full feeding sometimes hath crept upon Thy servant"—*Confessions* 10.31, trans. J. G. Pilkington (TinyURL.com/Augustine-10).

culture of the time, and the New Testament moral warnings reflected the Roman culture, which was completely different. Laws that reflect the culture of the time are unlikely to be timeless. Another indication that this law is not timeless is that the laws changed greatly with time: from constraining someone who was rebellious and uncontrollably destructive to warnings against the type of overindulgence that will lead to immorality.

CONSTRAINING GREED

This doesn't mean that we should dismiss what the two Testaments say. Although they clearly have different purposes, we should take both of them seriously. In some cultures, greed can rob others of the necessities of life, and the Old Testament shows that this greed has to be constrained. However, we no longer use force to do this; we now employ laws and taxes to influence people's consumption. And the New Testament warnings about parties where nothing was off-limits are particularly pertinent in Western societies. Also, greed for money and power has to remain one of the most serious sins. However, overeating itself is not regarded as sinful in the Bible, and it only became a sin when the church was influenced by asceticism in the early centuries.

Nowadays, our view of gluttony is similar to that in Proverbs 23:21: "Drunkards and gluttons become poor, and drowsiness clothes them in rags." We regard it as a moral failure that will lead to ill health, if not poverty. We celebrate things by having a big meal and look for something to eat as soon as we feel the slightest hunger. And we also constantly try to lose weight. All this implies a self-centered approach: we eat and we diet. The ancient world was more community based: greed was bad if it robbed the poor of scarce food, and mealtimes were good because they were social occasions for cementing friendships.

We could apply that community principle today if Christians decided to *only* eat when in company and regularly invite poor friends (who are often also lonely) to those meals. This would solve a lot of problems—for ourselves and others.

22

▾

Can You Ever Tell a Lie?

Do we criticize the magi for not telling Herod about the baby, as they'd promised? Ananias and Sapphira's lie got them killed. Is perjury different? Must your yes always mean yes?

I have a personal problem that causes suffering for all my family. They sometimes face endless interrogations and questions of clarification from me, often with increasing exasperation. The problem is that my mind can't be at peace with conflicting assertions—that is, I have an almost visceral reaction against inconsistencies. I know this isn't normal, and most people can't understand what the fuss is about. One side effect of this curious (dis)ability is that I can see how frequently people lie to themselves. However, I have discovered that helping them recognize this fact is rarely welcomed!

We all lie, and this is a normal aspect of being human. Our bodies even highlight our lies to help listeners recognize them. Our blink rate rises, tiny blushes and microexpressions furrow our face, and our vocal cords tighten a little. None of these are distinct enough for certainty, but we subconsciously register any accompanying statements as questionable.

Schools now teach children how to judge the reliability of websites and other sources of information. But sometimes even our cherished guardians of truth fail us. The UK's communications regulator, Ofcom, fined the BBC for various offenses including rigging elections: the children's program "Blue Peter" had a cat that should have been called "Cookie" because this got more votes from children than the proclaimed winning name "Socks"; and the vote for the best Bollywood actress was rigged because the winner wasn't available for an interview.[1]

President Trump has made us all aware that some people have different concepts of truth. We have gradually realized that he simply isn't ashamed to be caught lying; he even boasted that he made up "facts" during international negotiations.[2] But we should admit that he merely does candidly what most leaders do with more subtlety. When official government papers are released after a few decades, they often reveal truths that couldn't be admitted previously.

Sometimes we just *have* to lie. Rahab lied to save the lives of the Israelite spies (Josh 2:4–6), but sometimes we feel the need to lie in much less serious situations. A friend of mine met a colleague at a college dinner who appeared to be heavily pregnant, so he said: "Congratulations!" She asked: "What for?" He suddenly realized that she must have simply put on a lot of weight, so he said: "I heard you were offered a lectureship. ... No? Oh, I must have been mistaken." As he said to me, what else could he do?

LEGAL LIES AND SOCIAL LIES

God clearly takes lies seriously in the Bible. Even the pagan prophet Balaam recognizes that God's very nature is truthful

---

1. "BBC Fined over Contest Deceptions" (TinyURL.com/BBC-Lied).

2. Trump asserted the US has a trade deficit with Canada and later boasted at a rally that he'd made it up—see Josh Dawsey, Damian Paletta, and Erica Werner, "In Fundraising Speech, Trump Says He Made Up Trade Claim in Meeting with Justin Trudeau" (TinyURL.com/LiedToTrudeau).

("God is not human, that he should lie"), and the prophet Samuel agreed with almost identical words (Num 23:19; 1 Sam 15:29). God seems to be incapable of lies, because when he wanted to give some prophets a false message, he had to use a lying spirit to do so. That's how the prophet Micaiah explained the contrary message of his rivals (see 1 Kgs 22:19–23).

Lying is criticized throughout the Old Testament, though there is a clear distinction between social lies (Hebrew *kastav*) and legal lies (*sheqer*). The psalmist concludes that all humanity tells social lies, that is, untruths to family or neighbors ("Everyone is a liar"; Ps 116:11). However, legal lies are much more serious, that is, lying as a witness on oath or officially reporting someone's words wrongly—as when a prophet misreports God's message (e.g., Jer 5:31; 14:14).

Punishments for lies depend on their motive and effect. If you defrauded someone, you paid back 120 percent of the value, plus a guilt offering for having sworn falsely (Lev 6:1–7). And if you accused someone falsely, then you suffered the punishment they would have received (Deut 19:16–21). So if you lied about them killing someone, you'd get the death penalty! Most seriously, if you lied in a legal setting by making a vow in God's name, or even by keeping silent, there was no sin offering that could remove your guilt: "he shall bear his iniquity" and "the Lord will not hold him guiltless" (Lev 5:1; Exod 20:7 ESV).

But there is no punishment for social lies. Actually, they aren't even singled out for criticism in the Old Testament. All the laws and moral injunctions are aimed at legal lies. For example, the ninth commandment outlaws "false witness"—the word translated "false" is *sheqer*, which refers to legal lies, and this meaning is emphasized by adding the word "witness." These legal lies are criticized very frequently, but there aren't any texts that specifically criticize social lies.[3] Personally, I find this perplexing.

The New Testament takes lies much more seriously. When Ananias and Sapphira promised to donate to the church money that they received for a property they sold and lied about the amount, they dropped dead. We can see this as a special case because the Holy Spirit had just been given, and it says they had "lied to the Holy Spirit" rather than to church leaders (Acts 5:3). However, it does suggest that truthfulness was being raised to a higher level in the early church. When we get to the end of the New Testament, liars are listed among the murderers and rapists (Rev 21:8; 22:15).

Jesus established higher standards with regard to lies, as with many other morals. He warned against anger because it can lead to murder, and against sexual fantasy because it can lead to adultery (Matt 5:21–22, 27–28). In the same chapter Jesus warns against affirming truth with an oath, because this implies you allow yourself to lie on other occasions. "All you need to say is simply 'Yes,' or 'No'; anything beyond this comes from the evil one" (Matt 5:37).

In the Jewish world of Jesus' day, similar oaths to "on my mother's life" were used, but much more commonly. Making an oath in God's name was risky—because you *had* to keep it (see Deut 23:21), so instead they made oaths "by the Temple," or "by my head" (that is, "by my life").[4] But Jesus, like some other Jews,

---

3. Legal lies (*sheqer*) are criticized in Exod 20:16; 23:1, 7; Lev 6:3, 5; 19:12; Deut 5:20; 19:18; Pss 63:11; 101:7; Prov 12:22; 14:5; 19:5; 30:6; Jer 20:6; 23:32; 27:15; Zech 5:4; 8:17; 13:3; Mal 3:5. There are no specific criticisms of social lies (Hebrew *kastav*) except on the couple of occasions where the word describes legal lies— i.e., Prov 14:5; Ezek 13:19; Mic 2:11.

4. See Mishnah *Keritoth* 1:7 for "by the Temple" (TinyURL.com/mKeritoth -1-7); Babylonian Talmud *Berakhot* 3a for "by your head" (TinyURL.com/ bBerakhot3a). For more details, see Jacob Mann, "Oaths and Vows in the Synoptic

thought this was wrong.[5] For example, Simeon ben Antipatris (who lived roughly at the time of Jesus) had some visitors and invited them to stay for a meal. They said something like: "By the Torah, we certainly won't impose on you"—that is, they made an oath on the Bible. However, when Simeon asked a second time, they acquiesced and stayed. So Simeon gave them a meal, and then beat them with a rod for misusing a sacred vow.[6]

Some people interpret Jesus' teaching to mean that you shouldn't take an oath in court. But Jesus wasn't denigrating oaths—he was teaching that *every* oath is serious, because it is a promise before God to speak the truth. He was teaching his followers against using unnecessary oaths. They probably asked Jesus: "So how will people know that we are telling the truth?" He said: "All you need to say is simply 'Yes' or 'No'" (Matt 5:37). In modern times he would say: "Don't add 'really' or 'honestly'; just tell the truth every time."

EVERYBODY LIES

The sad truth is that humans do lie, both to others and often to ourselves. We even tell ourselves that we never lie, and yet we compliment an old person on how young they look, an ill person on how well they look, and a young child on how grown up they look. No one is harmed or fooled, and they are pleased with these social lies. We also tell lies to ourselves: we deserve a treat or a rest because we have worked harder than normal, when actually it has been an average day. Depending on whether

---

Gospels," *American Journal of Theology* 21 (1917): 260–74 (TinyURL.com/Mann -AJT21).

5. Josephus reports that the Essenes thought this way in *War* 2.8.6 (TinyURL .com/JosephusOaths), and 2 Enoch 49:1 says something very similar to Matt 5:33–37.

6. Babylonian Talmud *Derekh Eretz Rabba* 6 (TinyURL.com/Derekh EretzRabba6).

we are generally optimistic or pessimistic, we tell ourselves that we have certainly done well or done badly, or we are better or worse looking than someone else—when really we can't know. We are just fooling ourselves.

Social lies can, of course, be harmful, and often intentionally. Our lies can undermine someone's reputation or confidence and can ruin friendships with others, or they can promote our own reputation higher than warranted. But truths can also be used maliciously and be just as harmful as a lie. The evil of social lies comes not from the lack of truth but from the motive of malice or selfishness with which they are made. And when truth is spoken with that same motive, it is just as evil.

By contrast, legal lies are always harmful. If you tell a lie in court, it is always wrong.

Might an occasion arise when you have to lie to prevent greater harm? The rabbis thought this through and concluded that all the commandments can be broken in order to save someone from death, sexual assault, or forced idolatry.[7] So the wise men were right to break their promise to report back to Herod, and you can lie to terrorists and rapists to protect potential victims. This isn't stated in the Bible, but I think it is very wise.

The command against legal lies (false testimony) is changeless through the Bible, and although it is culture reflecting, it is a universal command. No society could function without it. Surprisingly, there is no command in the Bible against social lies, though I wish there were, because I find any lies difficult to cope with. Instead, humans are contrasted with God: although he is true, everyone else is a liar at some time or other (Rom 3:4).

---

7. All commands can be broken in order to save a life except the commands against idolatry, sexual immorality, or murder. See, e.g., Babylonian Talmud *Ketuvot* 19a (TinyURL.com/bKet19a).

My problem is that I have difficulty distinguishing between the legal lies and social lies, or harmful lies and harmless lies, without thinking hard. So personally, I recommend an easy practice: simply speak the truth. There are times, of course, when honesty can cause as much harm as a lie, so as an older generation wisely taught: if you can't say something nice, say nothing at all.

23

▾

Crude Language

The Bible has many phrases we can't translate literally because they'd cause offense or giggling. Some authors, like Paul, use offensive language we'd consider too strong today, though they don't use gratuitous violent or sexual terms merely to shock, as is common today.

The Bible contains a surprising amount of crude and offensive language, and our translations sometimes have to modify this. Imagine a respectable elderly lady in her cashmere cardigan reading from the pulpit Bible in church: "She lusted for lovers who had the penis of an ass and ejaculated like a horse" (a literal translation of Ezek 23:20). Friends of the brash new king Rehoboam advised him to emphasize that he was tougher than his father Solomon by telling the people: "My little finger is thicker than his penis" (1 Kgs 12:10, my translation). Translators have a tough time with that one!

I sit on an international Bible translation committee, and we often have to deal with issues like this. Sometimes a word is perfectly respectable in one society but not in another. One American translation that was going to be sold in England described the coast of Tyre as "a place to spread fishnets" (Ezek 26:5). My daughter (who was helping to proof it) said her jaw dropped open when she read that verse. In the US, "fishnets" catch fish, but in the UK they are sexually provocative stockings.

I remember one afternoon when the committee went through every instance of "booty" in the Bible, changing it to "plunder" or "looting"—and no one around the table would explain to me why we were doing it! The meaning of the word changed in North America and reached England later, so it was obvious to the American scholars. I had to ask one of the rougher kids in church back home to explain it.

Many aspects of language change with time. The King James Bible was able to translate literally the recurring Hebrew phrase "any that pisseth against the wall," but most modern translations modify this to "any male" (e.g., 1 Sam 25:22, 34). In the gentle days of my youth, church leaders were concerned to protect us from verses in the KJV that used "bloody" (e.g., Ezek 22:2) or "shut up" (e.g., Lev 13:4). In those innocent days we didn't even notice the potential problems in Luke 17:34–35: "There shall be two men in one bed ... two women shall be grinding together."

"IT WAS ALL CRAP"

The Bible occasionally contains deliberately offensive language. Paul directed some crude and angry words at his opponents who demanded that Christian converts be circumcised. He told them to go all the way and castrate themselves (Gal 1:12). And when he wanted to contrast his old religiosity with the new life he'd found in Christ, he said (in modern equivalent language): "It was all crap compared to Christ" (Phil 3:8). The word he chose (*skubalon*) wasn't a polite word like "feces" but a crude word that is found in ancient graffiti. He *wanted* to shock people out of their comfortable religion.

Jesus used offensive language when criticizing the religious establishment. He called them hypocrites, children of hell, blind fools, and snakes—to their faces! (Matt 23:13–17, 33). By this stage in his ministry there had been many opportunities for them to recognize Jesus as the Messiah, sent by God, but they were too set in their ways. In exasperation he publicly insulted them, trying to shock them into recognizing their faults, then went on to lament over the stubbornness of Jerusalem in not turning back to God (vv. 37–38).

There is even some blush-worthy language attributed to God. In Isaiah he says even our righteous acts are as filthy as used menstrual pads—usually translated coyly as "filthy rags" (Isa 64:6). This is deliberately meant to shock. Then at other times euphemisms are used, such as the shaming of the Assyrians by metaphorically being shaved by God, who will cut off the hair from their head, from their beard, and from their "feet" (Isa 7:20). To understand this euphemism you have to know that urine is called "foot water" (2 Kgs 18:27 = Isa 36:12).

Euphemisms have their place, making it possible to talk in a nonthreatening manner about matters that might cause embarrassment. However, we have gone to silly extremes. In polite society we even create euphemisms for "toilet" or "lavatory," such as "restroom" or "ladies' room." And yet the originals are already euphemisms—*lavare* is Latin for "washing," and a *toilet* is an old French word for a "cloth," indicating a dressing room.

Martin Luther's *Table Talk* is a fascinating record of Christian mealtime conversations in an earlier century. However, it is often cringe inducing to read, because no modern-day clergy would let themselves go into print with such crude and forthright language. Similarly, King James, when speaking to a conference of clergy to promote his new Bible, said to a group of Puritans: "I give but a turd for your argument."

Of course, you can be just as offensive using perfectly "good" language—politicians do it all the time. In many parliamentary chambers, politicians are constrained by a list of "unparliamentary language" that includes calling anyone a "liar," a "hypocrite," or "drunk." But these restrictions merely result in creative uses of language such as "he was as tired as a newt."[1] British politics was much livelier in the past, especially when Winston Churchill argued with Lady Astor, a former American citizen who became the first woman to serve in the UK Parliament. She once said to Churchill: "If you were my husband, I would feed you poison," to which he retorted, "If you were my wife, madam, I would take it!"[2]

Arnold Schwarzenegger was much loved as governor of California because he used phrases such as "economic girlie-man," and Donald Trump has a similar talent for offending people without using any officially banned language. A sadly neglected principle of politics is "attack the policy, not the person." Adversarial debates are sterile because no one is seeking to understand the opposite side. They want to win the debate rather than learn from it or come to a consensus.

At the other end of society, crude and violent words pepper conversations until they become mere punctuation. One of the worst examples is in a movie I love, *Midnight Run*, which pokes fun at this habit with a memorable line: "I have just two words for you: Shut the f*** up." This type of crude language, intended to offend or insult, is not helpful. If you use swear words in everyday speech, what is left when you wish to demonstrate anger or disgust?

Suppose you see drug pushers trying to sell to kids outside your children's school. Do you ask them politely to move along or tell them roundly what you think of them and their trade?

---

1. "Debates of the Legislative Assembly for the Australian Capital Territory: Hansard," December 14, 1995 (TinyURL.com/TiredAsNewt on p. 3049).

2. "Winston Churchill's Finest Quotes (3/11)" (TinyURL.com/ChurchillAstor).

SALTY, NOT GRITTY

Strong language does have a valuable function and is effective if it accurately communicates emotion or urgency, but this can only happen if it is used sparingly. Paul said: "Let your conversation be always full of grace, seasoned with salt" (Col 4:6). Paul was probably making a reference to the way that offerings in the Temple were seasoned with salt (Lev 2:13). This is completely opposite to what we mean by salty language, which normally refers to the colorfully rough language of sailors.

However, the ancient realities about salt actually make it an apt way of describing strong language. The salt of the ancient world also illustrates the danger of language that intends nothing but offense. Salt was one of the strongest sources of flavor, but unlike modern salt, it could also lose its flavor, as Jesus warned (Matt 5:13 = Mark 9:50 = Luke 14:34).

Salt was mostly mined and wasn't purified by washing, dissolving, and evaporation, as it is now. So if salt was left in a damp bag, the flavor gradually leached out, leaving nothing but the sandy impurities. If you then used this flavorless salt, it merely added grit to a meal. This is like using gratuitously offensive language instead of appropriately strong phrases. Instead of adding a little spice to enhance your reply to someone, you end up adding nothing but grit that makes their teeth grind. Those words will produce harm without adding anything interesting or wholesome.

Paul wasn't commending uniformly bland and inoffensive speech, but he invited us to think before we speak. In the Bible, crude language is used to make a forceful point or create a memorable analogy. Sometimes we need to genuinely demonstrate our anger or disgust. At those times, we should ask ourselves: Will my words inform and motivate the recipient, or will they act like grit, resulting in nothing but increased friction and bitterness?

Section 6

▾

For the Sake of Others

24

▾

Visiting Prisoners

Jesus listed visiting prisoners among the marks of a Christian life. Many people seek God in prison, but few Christians consider this a suitable place to work for God.

I have a relative whom I've never met and whose name I don't even know. Actually, I'm not even sure whether he exists or is still alive. He's someone no one ever talks about, except in whispers I overheard as a child. My best guess is that he was in prison and was disowned by the family, but the generation who kept that secret are now gone, so perhaps I'll never know. On the other hand, another relative of mine is very open about his time in prison—because he became a Christian there.

Prison is a very common experience. About one in ten men in the US spend some time in prison.[1] About a fifth of those in prison are awaiting trial, and about a fifth of these will be found not guilty,[2] so there are a lot of innocent people in prison. I'm not suggesting that no innocent people should ever be in jail—sometimes it is necessary to secure someone who might abscond before trial, and sometimes mistakes are made.

---

1. 9 percent of US men (according to TinyURL.com/JailRisk).

2. 21.5 percent of US prisoners are on remand, and 20 percent of them are not convicted (table 1 and footnote 9 at TinyURL.com/NotGuiltyRemand).

However, it does help to remind us that those who are locked up are human and just like us.

However, the prison population is also different from the average population in some surprising ways. About one in six prisoners suffer psychiatric delusions, compared to one in twenty-five in the general population,[3] and almost half of them have low reading skills,[4] which makes it difficult to hold down a job. There are all kinds of reasons people go to prison, and sometimes they are just too confused or ill-educated to do the right thing or to present the right information for their defense.

PRISON IN THE BIBLE

In Old Testament times, very few people were imprisoned because prisons didn't exist. Making a building impregnable enough to hold a prisoner was very difficult. When they did build something that secure, it was usually the house of a rich man or a leader. Of course, the house of a king could have dungeons, so a few high-profile criminals stayed there while being interrogated or simply waiting for execution on a day suitable for the king. Other criminals weren't imprisoned—they were simply executed when they were found guilty.

It is therefore surprising that quite a number of Bible characters spend time in prison. Joseph was in prison for supposedly raping Potiphar's wife, and while there he met two servants of Pharaoh—one was eventually reprieved and the other was executed, with no explanation (Gen 40:20–22). Samson arguably deserved prison after he had killed more than a thousand men who wanted to punish him for burning their fields (Judg 15:4–5,

---

3. TinyURL.com/PrisonMentalHealthUSA.

4. 46 percent have literacy skills at or below that of an eleven-year-old in the UK in 2015 (TinyURL.com/PrisonSkillsUK).

9–10, 14–15; 16:21), and perhaps Kings Zedekiah and Jehoia-
chim deserved imprisonment as sinful leaders whom the Lord
allowed to be defeated (2 Kgs 24:12; 25:7, 27–30). However, Daniel
and his three friends didn't deserve imprisonment for refusing to join in with pagan religions, and the prophets Jeremiah,
Micaiah, and Hanani were imprisoned because the king didn't
like the message God gave them (Dan 3:12–23; 6:10–16; Jer 37:15;
2 Chr 18:25; 16:10).

In New Testament times, there were more prisons and more
prisoners, especially under the efficient judicial system of the
Romans and their surrogates, which included Jewish leaders. At
different times, those prisons held John the Baptist, Peter, the
other apostles, Paul, and Silas (Matt 14:3; Acts 5:17–18; 16:22–24).

When we first meet Saul (who later became the Christian
Paul), he is incarcerating ordinary Christians. He put so many
people in prison that the Jerusalem Christians fled and scat-
tered to other cities throughout the country (Acts 8:1–3). Of
course, this had the opposite effect from what he was hoping
for, because the gospel spread with them.

The pastor of a Zimbabwean friend of mine was imprisoned
for speaking out against President Robert Mugabe. The prisons
were so overcrowded with similar "criminals" that he was in a
large, overcrowded cell with dozens of other prisoners. After
some months, he asked his church to help bribe the guards—not
to get him better treatment, but to go into another, similar cell,
because all the non-Christians in his old cell had found Jesus.

FINDING JESUS

Prison is a great place to find Jesus. A friend of mine in Cambridge offered to work in a prison as a chaplain and found that
prisoners were very receptive to the gospel. Of course, many
were just as resistant as they were outside, but others were much

more open. They didn't need convincing that something was wrong with their lives, and they had plenty of time to think about the good news he shared with them. After some time, a significant number of people had become Christians, and the prison governor offered him a full-time paid post because he needed fewer guards in the wing he'd been working in.

Paul, of course, spent a lot of time in prison. Some might see it as natural justice after sending so many people to prison in his former life as a persecutor of Christians. However, he rejoiced because he was able to spend time writing, and we have at least five letters he wrote from prison (Phil 1:12–18; Eph 3:1; Col 4:18; Phlm 9; 2 Tim 2:9). Actually, I think Paul was rejoicing through gritted teeth, because it must have been frustrating to be stuck in one place when he had helped spread the gospel through so much of the Roman Empire. If only he'd known how important those letters were going to be! He didn't realize that people would study his words in far more detail than any country's constitution or speeches made by any national leader throughout history.

God can use prison, but not without the action of his people. Paul needed people to visit him in prison, to bring him news and deliver letters. People who become Christians in prison need help growing in faith and understanding how to live their new life—and they will need help when they come out. But visiting prisoners is not just about adding people to the kingdom. It is also an expression of Christian love to those in need.

Christians help the homeless, the sick, and those in prison because these people need help, and because Jesus expects this. In Jesus' most terrifying parable—the sheep and the goats, told just before his arrest and imprisonment—he characterized the sheep as those who helped him: "I needed clothes and you clothed me, I was sick and you looked after me, I was in prison and you came to visit me." When the goats protested that they'd never seen Jesus in these situations, he said: "Whatever you did not do for one of the least of these, you did not do for me" (Matt 25:31–46).

Some interpret this parable as referring only to good done to Christians because Jesus refers to those in trouble as his "brothers." But this would contradict the rest of Jesus' teaching, such as: "Your Father in heaven causes ... his sun to rise on the evil and the good. ... If you love ... only your own people, what are you doing more than others? Do not even pagans do that?" (Matt 5:45–47). Christians don't only help those who are Christians or who might convert. The criterion isn't whether they are interested in Jesus, but whether Jesus is interested in them.

THE TEST OF A CHRISTIAN

Does this command still apply to us? We can't apply the test of seeing whether it remains the same throughout the Bible because there is no similar expectation to visit prisoners in Old Testament times, when prisoners were so rare. However, we can apply the test of whether this command is countercultural. It was not common to visit those in prison unless you were a relative or close friend. Prisoners often depended on visitors to bring food or bribe guards to give them an easier time. But you would not do this for someone you weren't close to, because visiting a prisoner brought suspicion on you.

The idea that anyone would visit a stranger in prison was unthinkable in that society, and yet Jesus says this practice is the test of a real Christian—it separates the sheep from the goats.

Although there are Christian organizations working in prisons, this is a neglected area for many Christians today. I find this strange because Jesus specifically encouraged this work. But perhaps it isn't too surprising because, after all, I'm one of those who has never been involved in this ministry. Prisoners are out of sight and out of mind—we have largely forgotten about them. But Jesus hasn't.

▼

25

Disappearance of Hospitality

Roman houses were designed as much for guests as for residents, and Jews regarded hospitality as a moral necessity. Early Christians encouraged each other to excel in this. And now we barely invite anyone in for coffee—has something gone wrong?

I f I were asked what "Britishness" is, I'd suggest it used to be "being fair" and now it is "being tolerant." In similarly simplistic ways, we might characterize Germans as "being industrious," the French as "living to the full," and the Italians as "looking good." In New Testament times, the Romans borrowed culture from the Greeks, for whom the most admirable quality was "being hospitable." Homer's epic poems the *Iliad* and the *Odyssey* (from the eighth century BC) include lots of stories where hospitality is rewarded, and bad things happen if it isn't offered or is misused. Even the war with Troy starts when hospitality goes wrong, because Paris goes off with Helen—his host's wife.

Roman homes were designed for hospitality, though from the outside they looked rather inhospitable. Very few windows looked outward, and the entrance had a porter to turn away undesirables. But once inside, you found a spacious lobby opening to a courtyard with doors and windows to all the surrounding rooms. They had fountains and plants to cool the air, and lots of seating because this was the most comfortable area before air conditioning. A rich person would have audience rooms and dining rooms for various types of visitors and occasions. If you weren't rich, the surrounding rooms would be filled with your extended family, who all lived and ate together in the evening, and it was normal to invite visitors.

This Greek and Roman emphasis on hospitality was something that Jews could agree with. They placed the same value on hospitality to strangers that many nomadic Arab tribes still honor—they welcome a traveler without hesitation.

ENTERTAINING ANGELS

In the area of hospitality, Abraham is the role model for both Jews and Arabs. When he saw three strangers some distance from his tent, he ran to greet them (despite it being very hot) and persuaded them to eat with him. He organized bread, cheese, and milk while they waited for the lamb to roast. He didn't talk with them about their business until after they'd eaten—which was a rule in Greek culture too.[1] In Hebrews 13:2 we read the moral of this story: "Do not forget to show hospitality to strangers, for by so doing some people have shown hospitality to angels without knowing it." Two of those three strangers turned out to be the two angels, who continued on to visit Lot, and the third appears to have been God in some physical manifestation, because Abraham "remained standing before the LORD" (Gen 18:22).

The first sign that something was terribly wrong in Sodom was the way they treated strangers. No one offered these angels hospitality except Abraham's nephew Lot. The story of this rejection would have reminded non-Jews about the ancient story of the Greek gods Zeus and Hermes in which they were refused hospitality by everyone except one poor couple. They

---

1. See TinyURL.com/WikiXenia.

were rewarded while all their neighbors were killed. This story was in the consciousness of many people even in Paul's day, because he and Barnabas were mistaken for these two gods when they healed someone (Acts 14:8–13).

Some stories in the Gospels make more sense when we realize the importance of hospitality. Getting your neighbor out of bed to lend you food for a midnight supper seems ludicrous—unless you have found someone who needs hospitality (see Luke 11:5–8). And the revealing of Jesus' identity to the pair going to Emmaus occurred after they invited him in for a meal—perhaps because a stranger wasn't required to state their name or business until you had given them food. Jesus was able to assume that his disciples would receive hospitality when he sent them to preach, and he even warned them not to take up a second offer if it was better than the first: "Stay there. ... Do not move around from house to house" (Luke 10:7). No, he wasn't forbidding door-to-door evangelism!

In contrast, no one gave up their room for Jesus' heavily pregnant mother. That's like refusing to give up your bus seat to an old woman struggling to remain standing. And when he became an itinerant preacher, Jesus was often refused hospitality. Samaritans refused because he also wanted to speak to Jews, and so many Jews refused him hospitality that he concluded, "Foxes have dens and birds have nests, but the Son of Man has no place to lay his head" (Luke 9:58).

Hospitality was especially important for Jews and Christians in the Roman-dominated world of the New Testament. Jewish dietary rules made staying in an inn very difficult. Christians sometimes had to stay with fellow Christians secretly because of persecution by Jews or by Romans. This wasn't problematic most of the time, but the emperors Caligula, Nero, and Hadrian were particularly paranoid, and even Jews could be considered dangerous sometimes. In Lystra, where Paul was mistaken for Zeus, he was talking to the crowds who wanted to offer sacrifices to him when some Jews arrived from nearby Antioch and persuaded the crowd to stone him instead (Acts 14:18–20). They almost killed him and yet, after preaching elsewhere for a while, he returned to encourage the believers in Lystra. Whoever gave him hospitality on that occasion was being as brave as Paul himself!

Peter, who wrote to a community suffering persecution, had to remind his flock to "offer hospitality to one another without grumbling" (1 Pet 4:9). The word for "hospitality" is *philoxenos*— that is, love of the stranger. It is opposite to "xenophobia," meaning "fear of the stranger," which we know all too much about today.

STUFF AS A HINDRANCE TO HOSPITALITY

The Bible only presents hospitality as an actual command with regard to fellow believers, but both the Old and New Testaments assume that hospitality will be shown to strangers too. This Bible teaching reflects the culture, which may imply that hospitality is not a timeless aspect of morality. However, this moral imperative remains the same throughout the Bible, which tends to imply that it is timeless. So we have one factor that implies that this is a timeless teaching and one factor that implies it may not be, because it aligns with the culture of the time. In this situation, we could only show that the teaching has changed if the culture has also changed. If our culture is very significantly different from that of Bible times, we have to conclude that God still requires his people to show hospitality to strangers.

One such difference in our culture does exist, and it is a very real and practical hindrance to our practice of hospitality. It isn't that we don't have enough food, or we don't have a spare couch.

It is that we own too many precious things and fear that they will be misused or stolen. It is a sad fact that those who have the least are the most likely to be hospitable. When a homeless person looks for a bed or a couch, they are much more likely to find hospitality in a one-bedroom flat than in a four-bedroom house.

So many of today's displaced immigrants are Christians, though there are also other religious groups fleeing hatred that has been stirred up in their home cultures. Jesus didn't call us just to love ourselves but to love our potential enemies and explained: "If you love those who love you, what reward will you get? Are not even the tax collectors doing that? And if you greet only your own people, what are you doing more than others? Do not even pagans do that?" (Matt 5:46–47). That last sentence cuts into my heart as a reserved British person. I might "love" a stranger, but surely that doesn't mean I have to be friendly to them! Jesus disagrees. If our love doesn't even extend to a friendly greeting, what kind of love is that?

Many in our grandparents' generation didn't lock their doors, and they knew their neighbors well enough to offer help when needed, as friends. In contrast, our generation complains that the government doesn't arrange enough help for elderly people who live alone—perhaps on our street. Our lonely neighbors usually only need coffee and a chat, and perhaps some shopping—which is much easier than the hospitality (that is, food and lodging) that the Bible expects us to give to complete strangers.

26

▾

Ending Slavery

Old Testament laws allowed slavery (within limits), and the New Testament allowed slave ownership (but not slave trading). However, the context shows God pushing society at each stage in one direction—toward abolition.

The church took a long time to outlaw slavery. You'd think it would have happened when Constantine became the first Christian emperor, but it continued for hundreds of years. In England, it wasn't until the time of William the Conqueror in the eleventh century that the fight against slavery really began to get started.

Perhaps one of the most devastating criticisms of the Bible is the accusation that it condones slavery and even that the Bible was to blame for its continuation. It is true that the Bible appears to sanction slavery because there are regulations about slavery in the Old Testament, and the New Testament has instructions to slaves to behave respectfully toward their masters. Paul even sent the runaway slave Onesimus back to his Christian master, Philemon, asking that he be treated well for Paul's sake (Phlm 15–18).

But it is a misunderstanding to believe that the Bible commends slavery. That the Bible regulates it doesn't mean that God approves of it. If it did, we'd conclude that our government commends all manner of child labor because it has so many laws that regulate it. These laws set limitations—children can't be forced to work, they must do so in a safe environment, they can only do certain types of work, and their hours of work are restricted. Just as child employment is not forbidden but highly controlled, the law of Moses strictly regulated the treatment of slaves, although it didn't prohibit slavery.

PART OF THE FAMILY

Slaves under the Old Testament law couldn't be ill-treated, had one day off per week (like everyone else), and had to be fed properly—it was even expected that they would eat with the family at feasts like Passover if they were circumcised (Exod 12:44). The medieval Jewish expert Maimonides said that early rabbis used to make sure their slaves ate first in case there wasn't enough food, because unlike family members, slaves had a legal right to that food.[1]

Most slaves in Israel were volunteers. That sounds like an oxymoron; however, in the days before banking, volunteering as a slave was the normal way to borrow money. If you needed a dowry for a daughter's marriage, you agreed with a local farmer to work for him for the next six years in return for your wages up front. During that time, you weren't given any pay (because you'd already received it), and the farmer was responsible for feeding and housing you—though he might not mind you sleeping at your own home. At the end of six years (the maximum allowed for this arrangement), some people decided they liked the work and the family life, so they asked to stay on; there was even a special ceremony for marking this (Deut 15:16–17).

---

1. Maimonides, *Mishneh Torah, Avadim* 9:8 (TinyURL.com/MaimonAvadim9).

Occasionally in the nation's history, the Israelites obtained slaves by defeating their enemies in nearby nations. The enslavement of these captives didn't end after six years, but they still had to be treated properly. If you hit your slave and knocked their tooth out, they could go free, and if you killed a slave, you were treated in the same way as if you'd murdered a free man (Exod 21:20, 27). Remarkably, a slave was allowed to run away from a master and find a better one—it was illegal to force a slave to return to a master (Deut 23:15–16). Of course, we know the Israelites didn't keep all of these laws all the time (they were sinners like we are), but these were the rules that God gave them to set them apart from other nations, whose treatment of slaves was very different.

PROPERTY, NOT PEOPLE

In New Testament times, Jews lived in the world of Roman law, which regarded slaves as property without any individual rights. After the fall of Jerusalem in AD 70, Jews passed a new law that forbade any Jew from ever becoming a slave, voluntarily or through debt. They also decided to treat non-Jewish slaves in accordance with Old Testament rules. Philo (a Jewish preacher in Egypt during Jesus' lifetime) said Jews should always remember that all men and women were equal in God's sight—and Paul used exactly the same terminology (Col 4:1).[2]

Paul couldn't go as far as telling Christians to release their slaves because it was illegal under Roman law to set free a slave who was younger than thirty.[3] Instead, he told them to treat slaves

---

2. Philo, *Special Laws* 2.68 (TinyURL.com/PhiloSpecial2).

3. Augustus made this limitation in *Lex Aelia Sextia* of AD 4 to prevent too many slaves being freed early. Census returns in Egypt and tombstones in Rome indicate that most slaves were indeed freed in their thirties. See more at TinyURL.com/LexJuniaNorbana.

with respect, like other workers, and if the slave was a Christian he was to be thought of as a "brother" (Phlm 16). Presumably, this "respect" included the normal Roman practice of manumission— that is, legally freeing them at age thirty so that they became proper Roman citizens with all of a citizen's rights and earning capacity. This practice was widespread, and some of the biggest and richest tombs along the Appian Way in Rome were built for slaves who founded thriving businesses after they were freed.

What Paul *could* do was to utterly condemn slave trading—as he did in 1 Timothy 1:10, which became the key text for Wilberforce's campaign to abolish slavery in the British Empire during the early nineteenth century. This condemnation is reiterated in Revelation, where slave traders are named among the evil members of a satanic empire that God will destroy (Rev 18:13).

GOD'S LONG-TERM PLAN

Instead of condoning slavery, the Bible shows us that God's plan was to gradually push the Jews and then Christians toward renouncing it, first by establishing rights for slaves and then by pointing out that all humans are equal (Gal 3:28). This should have resulted in the ending of slavery as soon as Christians had the political power to do so ... but it didn't happen like that. The church didn't recognize God's plan.

Any coach knows that you can't produce a perfect athlete in a single training session. You have to deal with each flaw gradually. This often means that coaches will put up with some faults while dealing with others because they have in mind the end of the process. Throughout the Bible, God is dealing with humanity in the same way, gradually showing us how to live with each other. Understanding his plan helps us understand the Bible. We shouldn't dismiss Old Testament law as irrelevant, nor should we view it as his final aim: it is a part of a process. Along with the New Testament, it forms God's training manual for societies and for individuals.

Some processes—such as the abolition of slavery—require a longer trajectory, so it is especially important that we recognize God's plan. Slavery and other ways of subjugating fellow humans were too ingrained to be abolished even by New Testament times. So the Bible states that the end point is equality for all humans and leaves the church to complete the process that has been started.

The laws about slavery are certainly not timeless. This is clear because they change between the Old Testament and New Testament. In the Old Testament, slaves were clearly not regarded as equal because they could not marry when they wished, and of course they had to do exactly as they were told. New Testament letters couldn't tell Christians to illegally free their slaves, but they were told to treat them as much as possible as equals: "Do not threaten them, since you know that he who is both their Master and yours is in heaven, and there is no favoritism with him" (Eph 6:9); "Masters, provide your slaves with what is right and fair, because you know that you also have a Master in heaven" (Col 4:1); "believing masters ... are devoted to the welfare of their slaves" (1 Tim 6:2).

Another indication that these laws are not timeless is that they reflect the culture of the time. The Old Testament laws were much more on the side of the slave than laws in surrounding countries, but they were nevertheless influenced by them, and New Testament rulings were constrained by the overwhelming might of Roman law. However, in both cases, the laws given to believers were pushing them in the same direction—toward treating all people, including slaves, as equal in God's sight. This shows us the timeless and eternal purpose of God to make us recognize equality in every human before God.

We perhaps fool ourselves into thinking that Western society has progressed so much further than the Old Testament. It is true that laws enshrine the right for each individual to be free, but there is no right for every individual to be fed and housed. Slaves had guaranteed housing, food, and, of course, work. Many individuals in modern society would love to be in the situation of ancient Israelite slaves.

Yet modern-day slaves are not in that position, and there is much more work to do in order for them to be free. Today, slavery is officially illegal throughout the world, but an estimated twenty-five to forty million people are still enslaved.[4] The problem and scope of international human trafficking is greater than it has ever been. Through movements like Stop the Traffik,[5] the church still has a vital role to play in helping to fulfill God's plan to bring freedom to all.

---

4. According to the International Labour Organisation; see TinyURL.com/ILO-Slavery.

5. www.stopthetraffik.org.

27

▾

Jesus' Effeminate Hair

Flowing, wavy locks were popular among promiscuous homosexuals in parts of Roman society, so Paul had to tell Christians to keep it short. Jesus probably did have long hair, but we can't be sure. Is there a rule that we should follow now?

When I was a teenager, as a joke I snuck into a formal photo of a girls' group at a summer camp. But when the picture was published, the joke was on me—my long, wavy hair made it impossible to guess that I was a boy! I clearly needed to cut it, but I didn't want a short back and sides—that was reserved for skinheads and the military—so I cut the sides short and kept the back long. It looked strange, but experimenting is what teenage years are for—and as wise parents say, hair grows back.

In New Testament times, experimentation like that could get you into trouble. Long, nicely groomed hair in adult men amounted to an advertisement for casual homosexual sex. As some first-century Jews said: "Long hair is not fit for men ... because many rage for intercourse with a man,"[1] and "the provoc-ative way they curl and dress their hair ... falsifies the stamp of

---

1. Pseudo-Phocylides XC–XCI (TinyURL.com/PseudoPhocylides), early first century AD.

nature."[2] Romans agreed—all the statues and portraits of men had short hair, except when they were depicting their enemies, who were often shown with long hair to make them look effeminate. Deliberately growing one's hair long to indicate you were open for male partnerships was especially popular among members of the Dionysian cult, who were famous for their alcohol-driven orgies. Perhaps they needed some very obvious markers that could be recognized even when you were drunk.

JESUS' HAIRDO

Did Jesus have long hair like he does in most of his modern portraits? Based on visual representations of Jews at the time, we can see that in Palestine things were possibly different from in the Roman world. Emperor Vespasian minted a coin in AD 79 to celebrate his victories against the Jews, depicting himself with a fashionable clean shave and short hair, while the reverse shows a defeated, kneeling Jew with long hair and a beard. Similarly, in a frieze on the Arch of Titus in Rome depicting the victory parade after the conquest of Jerusalem in AD 70, we find many short-haired Romans wearing victory laurels. Driven in front of their horses we see a young, beardless Jewish captive with hair falling over his shoulders. But these images might be part of the Roman habit of making their enemies look effeminate.

A picture of Jesus' baptism found in the Roman catacombs portrays him like a typical Roman—standing unashamedly nude, with a shaved chin and short hair. This was painted about AD 330, but a slightly earlier portrait of Jesus was discovered in 1963 in a Roman mosaic in Dorset, England. A Chi-Rho symbol (the first two letters of "Christ" in Greek) is behind his head where later generations would put a halo. He is clean-shaven,

---

2. Philo, *Special Laws* 3:36, 38, trans. C. D. Yonge (TinyURL.com/PhiloSpecial3).

but his hair is long and tied back, which was the fashion at the time the mosaic was made. In other words, Jesus is consistently portrayed like anyone else at the time of the artist, so these pictures give us no clue about his actual hairstyle.

Hair fashion was a huge problem at Corinth. This was a Roman city, and Romans were keen followers of fashion. They regarded their appearance as an indication of who they were. So when some Christian men wore their hair long, this was sending all the wrong signals to the Roman population, who regarded long hair as a signal of a promiscuous homosexual lifestyle. Paul had to remind them to cut their hair for the sake of the gospel. He didn't need to spell out why—he just had to point out that this was obvious and "natural": "Does not the very nature of things teach you that if a man has long hair, it is a disgrace to him?" (1 Cor 11:14). Any aging hippie would retort, "What's natural about a pair of scissors?" But Paul isn't arguing in the realm of logic—this was a clash of cultures.

Long hair was so disgusting on a Roman man that at first Paul can't bring himself to describe it in words. In verse 4 Paul says (translating word by word): "A man having down from his head is dishonorable." There's clearly something missing here, and most translations have unfortunately added something like "a head-covering," which is found in the early Latin translations. The correct word is supplied in verse 14—it is his "hair" that shouldn't hang down from his head. Paul was using a euphemism just like he did when describing the despicable sin of "a man [who] has his father's wife" (1 Cor 5:1 ESV). Has what?—has her eyes? or has supper with her? He politely omits to say "has intercourse with her," though we recognize *this* euphemism because we still use it. Of course, "intercourse" itself is a euphemism that originally meant "conversation." Like Paul, we frequently omit words when we don't want to offend.

Paul couldn't have meant that it was disgusting for a man to pray with his head covered because the opposite was true. Jewish men normally wore a prayer shawl, and Roman men pulled their toga over their heads when leading prayers. No man in Paul's day prayed with his head uncovered, and to do so would have been regarded as dishonorable to his deity. Even in the Old Testament the priests wore headgear (Exod 28:4), so there is no reason why Paul's readers would regard a covered head as dishonorable when praying.

HATS ON? HATS OFF?

The mistranslation (adding "head covering") led to centuries of banning men from wearing hats in church. The archbishop of Canterbury even vetoed broadcasting the wedding of the future George VI and Elizabeth in 1923 because some men might listen to it on the radio without removing their hats. This is still a cultural norm. Even though women no longer have to cover their heads in church, most men will still take off their hats— even those nailed-on baseball caps.

Hats for women were based on a similar misunderstanding. Paul, in his euphemistic style, criticized women who were (translating word by word) "with their heads uncovered" (1 Cor 11:5). What should they be covered with?—a veil, a shawl, a burka, an Easter bonnet? Whatever it was, it was obvious to everyone. Just as with men's hairstyle, everyone knew what was acceptable, so Paul merely had to say: "Judge for yourselves: Is it proper for a woman to pray with her head uncovered?" But covered with what? Here again, we find the answer in Roman culture and in a later verse.

Roman women never let their hair down in public—they kept it up on their heads, except when with their lovers and perhaps their intimate family—just as in Britain until the early 1900s. Wearing it down was equivalent to being partially undressed. Paul makes clear in verse 15 that the head should be covered with hair: "Long hair is given to her as a covering." Only prostitutes would ignore this rule. But his initial coyness in verse 5 means that here too the early Latin translations added the word "head covering" and constrained Christian women to wear hats in church for many centuries.

This was clearly an important issue for Paul and the early church. If long-haired men were seen taking a public role in the church by leading prayers, Roman visitors might reasonably conclude that casual homosexual sex was normal among Christians. This assumption was based on a prejudice, of course—even in Roman society it is possible there were men who wore long hair for reasons other than advertising for male lovers. But this prejudice was an unnecessary hindrance to the church, and Paul says they should avoid it. Similarly, women who wore their hair down in public were acting like prostitutes and causing a scandal to the church.

The Old Testament doesn't say much about hairstyles. Absalom, whom people appear to have regarded as handsome, used to cut his hair once a year—we are told his annual hair growth weighed five pounds, so it must have been lush (2 Sam 14:26). Apparently, it didn't matter whether hair was long or short. There was also an obscure regulation that is still taken very seriously by Hasidic Jews today: "Do not cut the hair at the sides of your head or clip off the edges of your beard" (Lev 19:27; 21:5). We can't be sure what this originally referred to: the context suggests it was a mourning rite, or perhaps it was because other desert tribes *did* do this (Jer 9:26; 25:23; 49:32). Or perhaps it was a law against personal grooming.

DOES IT HINDER THE GOSPEL?

These rules about hairstyles aren't timeless, as can be seen by the way they change with time, and they reflect culture. The Bible doesn't have timeless commands forbidding the carefully clipped beards of hipsters or the long, flowing hair of hippies. The purpose behind these rules is unclear in the Old Testament, but in the New Testament Paul appears to be telling believers to respect the rules of decency in fashion at the time. Men should not have hair long enough to flow down from their heads, and women should not let their hair down in public. Both of these styles were used in Rome by those who were advertising for casual sex. It was like wearing fishnet stockings or pinning a condom package to your lapel today.

So these rules are still relevant in that the *purpose* for that rule does still exist. We still have to ask ourselves: Is there any part of our lifestyle that hinders the gospel? If there is, then we should restrict our freedom so that others will be more able to hear the gospel without being put off by us. Paul said when he was asked why he restricted his personal freedom: "I am not seeking my own good but the good of many, so that they may be saved" (1 Cor 10:33). These early Christians were willing to restrict their freedom in all kinds of ways for the sake of the gospel, and they set us a very high standard.

28

▾

Improper Fashions

The Bible implies that some fashions are immoral. It appears to condemn tattoos, jewelry, and much more. Is this culture specific, or are these things still banned?

A friend's daughter popped into the living room to say goodbye before going out, but, distracted by an interesting book, he simply gave her a cheery wave without looking up. It was only the slamming of the front door, closely followed by his daughter stomping back into the room, that got his attention. "Why are you letting me go out looking like this?" she demanded. "It's indecent!" It took him some time to work out that she'd been relying on being able to tell her friends that he'd banned her from wearing the latest risqué fashion. Sometimes our kids need us to be their scapegoats.

Roman society took dress codes very seriously, and the rich spent huge amounts on their appearance. Rules about hair were particularly strict. Wearing a head covering or decorative bands to keep the hair up marked a woman's married status. An adult woman wouldn't be seen in public with her hair down, though it was acceptable among her intimate family and friends. If formal guests arrived, she would demurely pull up a loop of cloth that was lying across her shoulder like a scarf. Jewish society had the same sensibilities. It was said of one particularly pious woman,

Kimhith, that even her ceiling had never seen her hair![1] Only dancing girls, prostitutes, and loose women would let their hair down in public, and a demure woman would always keep it covered.

So why was the issue of hairstyles so controversial for the Corinthian believers? It seems the problem arose because they weren't sure whether the church meeting was a public or a private function. They probably met in the home of a rich member, so how were they supposed to act—like family friends (in which case a headdress wasn't strictly necessary, and you might even let your hair down) or like formal visitors? Paul's response was typically mindful of others: he said these meetings are public, so believers should be considerate of strangers (1 Cor 14:23). A modern parallel might be the wearing of a swimsuit. While most of us would find it perfectly decent for bikinis or swimming trunks to be worn at the beach on a hot day or around a private pool, we'd wear a bit more in church!

TRANSPARENT FABRICS

The Roman Empire's well-defined dress code meant that you could tell a person's rank and often their profession by the clothes they wore. A signature look for those of senatorial rank was a purple stripe on one's toga—which was strictly forbidden to anyone not in this elite group. The gladiators' fashion statement was their short leather tunics, which they wore even when they were off-duty to attract rich lovers. Well-off women had a wonderful range of materials to choose from. Intricate lace and expensive colored threads woven in complicated patterns were imported from the East or produced by house slaves. Embroidery was a skill that even rich women were proud to display, partly because it was a mark of matronly virtue that indicated

---

1. Babylonian Talmud *Yoma* 47a (TinyURL.com/bYom47a).

they weren't spending their time pursuing lovers. The fabrics ranged from dense woolen togas, which fell in clean, smart lines, to materials so sheer they were virtually transparent. These thin materials were worn as clothing by high-class prostitutes or as head veils by women who didn't want to obscure their expensive hairstyles. Spangled dresses were made by lavishly weaving real gold into the thread.

Conspicuous wealth was common, and the £20,000 per year that Princess Diana reputedly spent on hairstyling would have been considered penny-pinching in the highest strata of Roman society. Juvenal, a satirical comic of the second century AD, complained that these rich extravagances actually made them ugly, like the woman who "encircles her neck with green emeralds, and fastens huge pearls to her elongated ears."[2] The enormous amount of money spent on fashion was scandalous by any standard, and believers weren't immune to this temptation. Paul urged the believers to dress modestly and warned them against expensive hairdos, jewelry, and clothes (1 Tim 2:9). Peter wrote about this to believers living among Gentiles—and specifically to those in Rome. He warned women not to concern themselves with outward beauty, making an impression by braided hair, gold jewelry, and fine clothes (1 Pet 3:3–4).

A few believers today meticulously obey the New Testament commands on fashion, such as the Amish, who avoid all ostentatious jewelry and perms—even buttons are frowned on. I love that they can compliment each other by saying: "You look plain today!"

TATTOOS AND JEWELS

The Old Testament has a different set of rules. Men must dress as men, and women as women (Deut 22:5), and if you shaved

---

2. Juvenal, *Satire* 6 (TinyURL.com/JuvenalSatire6).

off a man's beard he'd be too ashamed to appear in public
(1 Chr 19:4–5). It was very important in all ancient societies to
know who was male and who was female, because a woman
alone with a man for just a few minutes was suspected of being
defiled. There were rules against tattoos and cutting yourself. This didn't refer to modern-day decorative tattoos and
skin scarification for decorative purposes—that is, patterns
made from scar tissue, which is particularly popular among
some African tribal groups. The ancient practices forbidden in
Israel's law were deformities and injuries you were expected to
make to demonstrate the depth of your mourning at a funeral
(Deut 14:1; Lev 19:28; Jer 16:6).

The Old Testament is surprisingly critical of rich people
flaunting their jewelry. Isaiah complains that "the women
of Zion are haughty, walking along with outstretched necks,
flirting with their eyes, strutting along with swaying hips,
with ornaments jingling on their ankles," and says that "the
Lord will snatch away their finery: the bangles and head-
bands and crescent necklaces, the earrings and bracelets and
veils, the headdresses and anklets and sashes, the perfume
bottles and charms, the signet rings and nose rings, the fine
robes and the capes and cloaks, the purses and mirrors, and
the linen garments and tiaras and shawls" (Isa 3:16–23). Amos
calls them "cows of Bashan ... who oppress the poor and crush
the needy and say to your husbands, 'Bring us some drinks!'"
(Amos 4:1).

SENDING THE WRONG MESSAGE

Most of the church has decided that none of these commands
are timeless—that is, we can ignore them. But is this true?
They didn't really change with time, except in emphasis. The
rule about cross-dressing in order to deceive didn't change—it

is just that no one needed to state it in New Testament times because Roman society was so sensitive about modes of dress that no one would consider it acceptable. Conversely, the rule about women keeping their hair up or covered was so ingrained in the ancient cultures of Old Testament times that there really was no need to say anything about it in the past. It was only in the first century, with its climate of women testing boundaries, that such a question would even arise.

However, all of these rules mirror the culture they were created for, which makes it much less likely that they are timeless. The custom of permanently deforming or scarring one's skin as a sign of mourning is no longer part of our culture. It is perfectly decent for a woman to be seen with her hair hanging loose—though this continued to be regarded as improper until relatively recently, so that "letting your hair down" still means to relax at home. Any nonhipster male can be seen beardless in public without feeling shame. And a prostitute can dress exactly the same as royalty (and vice versa), so it's difficult to see what all the fuss was about.

While we can ignore these specific commands, we shouldn't forget they had a purpose, and that purpose is a timeless message for us. Sexually provocative clothing can send the wrong messages in any culture, just as well as provocative actions by someone dressed demurely.

What concerned Peter and Paul mostly were displays of ostentatious wealth that included wearing expensive jewelry, clothes, and hairstyles. As well as demonstrating a worldly concern with outward beauty rather than inner holiness, this showed these women had little concern for the poor and needy. James, too, had some cutting remarks for believers who showed favoritism to the richly dressed over the poor (Jas 2:2–4). If the apostles were addressing today's church, they might have included warnings about flashy cars, trophy wives, and homes filled with the latest high-tech gizmos. This was about far more than fashion; Peter and Paul were criticizing all types of selfish squandering. It's a message that urges us to make sure we remember where our real treasure is.

29

▾

Eating Animals

Paul advised some Christians to become vegetarians because meat might come from animals killed as a sacrifice. Are there different issues today that might give a similarly bad impression?

My father encouraged many people to take up a vegetarian diet for their health, but he was a hypocrite—he secretly continued eating sausages and chops. In retrospect, I can't condemn him, because he may have helped those he advised. Anyway, in the end it was an herb that killed him—tobacco!

Eating a meat-free diet for health reasons is a recent innovation. The idea, and even the word "vegetarianism," didn't exist until the mid-1800s. Before that, a meat-free diet was known as "Pythagorean," after the Greek philosopher who, six centuries before Christ, rejected meat out of kindness to animals. Three centuries later, the Indian emperor Ashoka outlawed the killing of many animals that were used for food when he suddenly converted to nonviolence after decades of establishing his rule by ruthless massacres. But meat-free diets for health reasons had to wait until dietary studies discovered that eating a sufficient variety of nuts and vegetables supplies all the essential amino acids found in meat, without some of the less healthy fats.

None of this explains why vegetarianism among early Christians helped to avert a split in the church, or how Paul's response can help us avoid analogous problems today. But it does help to explain why Gentile converts at Corinth found the idea of vegetarianism so strange. Paul had to devote almost three chapters to this issue in his letters to Corinth and Rome (1 Cor 8; 10; Rom 14).

SOURCE OF MEAT

The problem was caused by Jewish Christians who said that you couldn't eat meat sold in an ordinary market because these carcasses were most likely from the various temples in the city. Very many offerings were made, and the priests couldn't possibly eat them all, so the majority were sold to butchers. Presumably, some meat came straight from farmers, but food labeling hadn't been invented, and no one cared except Jews and Christians. So Christians ended up eating animals that had been offered to idols.

Blood was also a problem because Jewish law said that it should all be drained from the carcass, and this was not the case with the meat found in Gentile markets. Special Jewish butchering techniques were needed to ensure that no blood remained. This only affected Jews, but this caused a rift between Christian Jews and Gentiles, so they had problems sharing meals. As a result, Gentile Christians were urged to avoid eating blood for the sake of harmony, which meant that both early Jewish and Gentile Christians tended to avoid any meat killed by Gentiles (Acts 15:20). They presumably did this by buying from Jewish butchers, which was fine—until they were suddenly banned.

Paul wrote at a time of anti-Jewish policies in the city of Rome. According to Jewish historian Josephus, these were provoked by some Jewish con men (see chapter 15, "Female Leaders"), though according to Roman historian Suetonius it was due to riots "instigated by Chrestus" (which may refer to Christ or Christians).[1] According to Acts, there had also been some Jewish-Christian riots in Corinth (Acts 18:12–17). So there were many reasons for anti-Jewish feelings, and an easy way for the authorities to punish Jews (and gain favor with the rest of the population) was by withdrawing licenses from all Jewish butchers in the city. This meant that Jews in Rome and Corinth couldn't buy kosher meat—and this also affected Jewish converts to Christianity.

Suddenly, a potential church split appeared over something that looked like nothing. Jews were keen on the idea of avoiding nonkosher meat because it felt heroic. All Jews remembered how Daniel and his friends had refused meat in Babylon and had turned out to be healthier as a result (Dan 1:12–16). But Gentile Christians couldn't see what the fuss was about, though they didn't mind buying from Jewish butchers when they could. The whole issue was all too complicated, and anyway, meat tastes good however it is killed.

Paul stood in the middle. He understood the way that Jews felt, but he agreed with the Gentile believers. He recognized that Jesus made the food laws irrelevant and could see that an idol "is nothing" (1 Cor 8:4–6). So while Jews banned any food that they weren't sure about,[2] Paul only refused meat if he'd been specifically told that it had been offered to an idol. His attitude was don't ask, just eat; because it all comes from God (1 Cor 10:25–26).

But what if you are at a meal with other Christians and someone says: "That meat has been offered to an idol, because it was bought from a butcher linked with the temple of Apollo; and that wine too—a drop of it was offered in the temple before the

---

1. Suetonius, *Life of Claudius* 25.4 (TinyURL.com/Suet-Claudius-25).
2. Mishnah *Demai* 4:1–2 (TinyURL.com/mDemai-4-1).

rest was sold in the same stall"? When someone tells you something like that, Paul says, you should act completely differently "for the sake of their conscience." If you simply go ahead and eat the meat, they might think you don't mind worshiping Apollo (1 Cor 10:19–20, 27–28).

Surely this is hypocrisy! Paul is playing the game of "don't ask, don't tell." He's doing one thing when some people are present, and then another when others are present. Paul admitted he was doing things differently when different people were present, but this wasn't hypocritical. He was limiting his freedom for the sake of his fellow believer who might stumble in his faith if he didn't (1 Cor 10:29–32). He even said that this was his attitude in other things too: "I try to please everyone in every way. For I am not seeking my own good but the good of many, so that they may be saved" (1 Cor 10:33).

THREE MORAL TESTS

Was Paul suggesting we should simply be yes-men about everything so that people will like us and respond to the gospel? He gives three reasons for his change in behavior, which suggest the kinds of situations where he would bend in this way:

1. *It might lead them into sin.* He warned the Corinthians, "If you think you are standing firm, be careful that you don't fall!" He reminded them that others who had gotten too close to idolatry had fallen into sexual immorality (1 Cor 10:7–12), especially if they actually ate meat in a pagan temple, as some of them were doing (1 Cor 8:10).

2. *It might bring the gospel into disrepute.* If someone saw Christians eating idol offerings, they might think they were idol worshipers. Paul says

that this might hinder others from being saved
(1 Cor 10:32–33).

3. *It might cause others to sin.* If other believers saw
them, they might think it was OK to worship idols
and fall into that sin themselves (1 Cor 8:9–13).

Paul concluded that those who had scruples about it—those
who felt that it was wrong in God's eyes—should not eat meat
because they would be disobeying what they felt God was telling them. But for those who didn't share these scruples, it was
OK, though he still felt that dangers for other people (as listed
above) made it inadvisable.

CLUBBING AND HALLOWEEN

There are many similar situations in the modern church where
some believers have scruples about something that others don't
share. For example, many believers regard Sundays as a day for
rest and recreation, so that shopping for pleasure is perfectly
OK, because the Sabbath laws were completely supplanted when
Jesus died (see Col 2:16). Others regard Sunday observance as a
continuation of Old Testament Sabbath laws and see shopping
as forcing someone else to work. Similarly, in some countries
Christians have taken a stand against alcohol, especially where
its abuse is endemic, whereas in other countries Christians feel
free to drink with moderation.

What if a Christian who felt freedom with regard to Sundays
and alcohol encouraged a Christian from an opposite culture to
join them in a bar on a Sunday? In one sense, no sin is committed, but the Christian from the less permissive culture will feel
guilty and will be going against her conscience.

The way to test whether something falls under this kind
of problem is to ask the question: What false though harmful

conclusion might someone come to if I do this? Here's a couple of examples: clubbing and Halloween. If a believer goes clubbing, someone might wrongly conclude that he is also sleeping around. If a believer joins in with Halloween celebrations, someone might wrongly conclude that she supports witchcraft or Satanism. To test whether to do these things, we can ask the three questions that Paul highlighted:

1.   Might it lead me into sin?

2.   Might it bring the gospel into disrepute?

3.   Might it cause others to sin?

Clubbing may be misunderstood if we are seen by someone who doesn't know us well, especially if our mode of dress reinforces their conclusion. And, in some cases, it may lead us into sin. This is something we have to consider very carefully. Halloween is rather different, because it is difficult to imagine how it could be the slippery slope to Satan worship or how someone could imagine that wearing a witch's hat means that we want to be one. However, it may imply that Christians don't take the evil one seriously.

When we come back to the issue that is actually addressed by Paul, we find it has little relevance to us today. Few communities still practice religious sacrifice, and they don't produce a surplus of meat so that it ends up in butcher shops. Eating meat has now become an issue for completely different reasons: personal health and animal welfare. Although these are both extremely serious issues, they are regarded as personal decisions, so there is no reason to change our behavior for the sake of other believers. I'm glad of this, because personally I agree with the gourmet Clement Freud, who reasoned: if you eat and drink sensibly all your life, you may not live longer—it just feels like it. However, Paul's discussion of the meat-eating issue provides us with some really useful guidelines that work for a wide variety of issues that affect us today. If we skip over chapters 8–10 in 1 Corinthians because the issue is no longer relevant today, we miss some really valuable teaching that provides guidance in all kinds of situations.

30

▼

Work, Even in Retirement

Our modern concept of retirement can make people feel useless. Paul encouraged the elderly to do useful work for their family or church.

"▐ dle hands" is the shorthand for an aphorism that was commonplace in my childhood: "The devil finds work for idle hands." The idea is that if you aren't doing any productive work, you are likely to fall into bad ways. This was so ingrained into me that even now I can't sit doing nothing without the question going through my head: What work should I be doing right now? It makes the idea of sitting on a beach quite unbearable, so the retirement I look forward to doesn't include much relaxation.

Others who struggle with burdensome and difficult work long to retire and loaf around. So they sit back—for a few months—and then they tend to look for something to do. It doesn't have to be "work," but something productive or helpful, or perhaps just more interesting than passively watching a screen.

FIND SOMETHING GOOD TO DO

I think Paul would have muttered something like "idle hands" when he saw people with nothing to do. In his first letter to the Thessalonians, he advised his young church: "You should ... work with your hands, just as we told you, so that your daily life may win the respect of outsiders and so that you will not be dependent on anybody" (1 Thess 4:11-12). Apparently, some people didn't do as he hoped, so in his second letter he was rather more blunt: "When we were with you, we gave you this rule: 'The one who is unwilling to work shall not eat.' We hear that some among you are idle and disruptive. They are not busy; they are busybodies. Such people we command and urge in the Lord Jesus Christ to settle down and earn the food they eat. And ... never tire of doing what is good" (2 Thess 3:10-13).

Notice that Paul was not just criticizing freeloaders who relied on others to feed them when they could have worked. He also encouraged those who weren't needy to "never tire of doing what is good." That is, find something good and worthwhile to do—such as feeding those who have little and can't work. One of the first programs the early church set up was a lunch club for widows. That's why the earliest church leaders were called "deacons," which is Greek for "waiters."[1] So Paul didn't mean that we should work until we drop—the church did cater for the elderly—but we should work while God gives us strength—that is, beware of "idle hands"! OK, he didn't actually say that, but that's the way he thought.

Part of Paul's motivation was, as he said, "that your daily life may win the respect of outsiders." Roman men were expected to do useful work even if they were rich. Rich men were encouraged to take on onerous administrative workloads by two devious schemes: first, you could only get a grand title such as "proconsul" if you accepted the work that came with it; and second, you could only apply for this title if you were rich enough. This meant that a social-climbing man would work really hard to earn enough money to qualify for a title, and then he would work hard

---

1. See Acts 6:1-2: "wait [*diakoneō*] on tables."

for the state in the role that went with that title without getting any wages. A clever system!

A Roman woman was also expected to work even if she owned enough slaves to do all the work of the house. Tombstones sometimes show women with a distaff—a cone-shaped object used for spinning a lump of sheep's wool into thread for weaving—and an actual distaff was often buried with a woman. This indicated that she was a respectable and industrious member of the household who continued to make or decorate clothing for her family, even if she had enough slaves to manicure her toenails while she weaved.

We see this mentality when Tabitha (aka Dorcas) died. Her life had been full of "doing good and helping the poor" (Acts 9:36), but when people appealed for Peter to pray for her, they didn't tell him about her social work. Instead, they showed him "the robes and other clothing that Dorcas had made" (Acts 9:39). These garments were the customary proof that she was a respectable, hardworking woman—though Peter didn't comment about which aspect of her life impressed him the most.

WOMEN TOO

Paul also expected women to work. He complained that some women—especially the younger widows—"get into the habit of being idle and going about from house to house ... busybodies who talk nonsense" (1 Tim 5:13). We wouldn't be surprised, after this apparently demeaning assessment of women, if he told them to spend their time making clothing. But he had a far more important task for them. (Not that he would have regarded weaving as a waste of time because, after all, his trade was making tents.) In the next verse he reminds these women of their most important role: they were expected to "manage their homes" (*oikodespoteō*—1 Tim 5:14). That is, they had the role of "master of the house" (*oikodespotēs*)—a term that is used for men when they manage their business (e.g., Matt 13:27; 20:1; 21:33) and used for women with regard to practical matters inside the home.

We see from this that Paul, like Romans of his time, regarded the woman of the house as its center and in some senses the boss. The distaff was her symbol, not only because she used it to spin wool, but because everything spun around her, and the household would fall apart if she didn't take charge. Paul extended her charge to the whole family—not just the children but also older dependents: "If any woman who is a believer has widows in her care, she should continue to help them and not let the church be burdened with them, so that the church can help those widows who are really in need" (1 Tim 5:16).

Some women could follow careers outside the home in a surprising variety of fields. They were needed for midwifery and baby care, but they were also able to do most of the things that men did. They commonly worked in farming, in craftwork, running market stalls, in laundry, in baking, or in making tents like Priscilla (Acts 18:1–3). Some women even succeeded in the "male" domains of oratory, writing poetry, and athletics; and there were even a few female gladiators.[2] The ideal woman of the Old Testament—the ideal presented in Proverbs 31— was an entrepreneur who traded and developed land, making enough money to support her husband in public office (Prov 31:14–24), as well as using the distaff (v. 19).

---

2. See the chapter "Women's Work" in Lynn Cohick's *Women in the World of the Earliest Christians: Illuminating Ancient Ways of Life* (Grand Rapids: Baker Academic, 2009). For the Jewish world, see Judith Romney Wegner, *Chattel or Person? The Status of Women in the Mishnah* (Oxford: Oxford University Press, 1988).

AND THE RICH

If rich people didn't hold any public office, they were at least expected to use their money for public good. As any philanthropist will tell you, managing financial support is time-consuming and sometimes tedious work. A rich Roman could be a patron of the arts by supporting a poet or a historian; or a patron of the city by designing and financing public offices or water supplies; or she could be a patron of the poor by paying for the corn dole, for which she might expect a public inscription in gratitude (which is how we know about this). Rich Christians had a different and arguably much more important way to be patrons: they could support apostles and evangelists.

One patron who supported Paul was Phoebe, and she was rich enough to support many others too (Rom 16:1–2). We don't know whether she had inherited wealth, but perhaps she worked as an exporter to Rome: she lived in Cenchreae—the port area of Corinth—and she apparently carried Paul's letter to Rome, perhaps while on a business trip (Rom 16:27 in some manuscripts, followed by the KJV). Another church patron, Lydia, was probably a luxury cloth dealer (Acts 16:14–15, 40). Sadly, no names of male patrons survive. I like to think that they were so common that they weren't noteworthy, though I fear that the early church had few patrons.

Neither the Old or New Testament had a concept of retirement, so although both of them show people working into their old age, this may not be an intentional message. It merely reflected the culture they were in. However, both Testaments suggest that those who were rich enough to be idle found useful work to do. This can't be regarded as a command, but it is certainly a moral message, since support is commanded for the poor, elderly, and sick.

Today, many of us have the privilege of planning for retirement. This means we can decide how to spend our resources of time, finances, and goods. We can regard them as our reward for working hard or as a gift from God to be used wisely. The most valuable asset is time—which perhaps we had very little of before we retired. In retirement from full-time work, we might not have the energy to do everything that we'd like, but we can support others through mentoring, giving, encouraging, and prayer. Time is something that can be wasted or spent—and during retirement we have absolute freedom to do either.

▼

What Next?

New ethical issues are arising that didn't occur in Bible times. This summary of techniques, validated by these worked-through examples, will help you navigate uncharted areas, using the Bible as a foundation.

This book started by outlining methods for extracting moral guidance from an ancient text, then examining real-life examples to see whether the theory actually works. The results in every chapter suggest that this method works remarkably well.

Often we have found that rules change with cultures, but this does not imply that the purposes behind these rules have also changed. In every case we have identified a consistent purpose, so that the Bible displays the same moral purpose throughout, from Old Testament to New.

Some examples that we examined were questions that are no longer issues in modern Western society, such as whether to allow polygamy or slavery and whether girls should be educated—although, as we know, there are problems with these issues in some parts of the world. Other examples concerned issues that haven't changed much since Bible times, such as sexual immorality, racism, lying, and crude language. Other issues are often thought to have changed, but we found that the difference is not so great after all, such as rules about homosexuality, divorce, fashion, abortion, or hospitality.

This method even solved some issues that have long caused problems in some parts of the church, such as people being barred from leadership positions because they are divorced, or women, or have rebellious children; wives who are taught to submit to their husbands in all things and risk being trapped in abusive relationships; and tolerance of homophobia and sexism.

SUMMARIZING THE METHOD

What these examples showed us is that the background context is the key. Without it, we are reading the equivalent of ancient replies to letters that are lost, so we don't know what they are responding to. We can't know whether the law of Moses is telling Israel to be more strict or less strict about something if we don't know what was normal in the surrounding nations. And we can't know whether Paul is telling people to fit in with Roman society or to take a stand against it if we don't know how Romans actually lived.

Here's a summary of the method outlined in the first section, as refined by the examples that we worked through:

1. We need to determine whether a particular rule in the Bible is timeless or not. That is, we need to discover whether it should apply at all times in all cultures (including our own) or whether different cultures require different rules. We determine whether a rule is timeless by asking two questions:

   - Is the rule the same throughout the Bible—for example, is it the same in both Old and New Testaments?

- Is the rule countercultural—that is, does it stand in contrast to the surrounding culture in the Old or New Testament?

If the answer to both is Yes, then it is very likely that this rule is timeless. The only exception is when culture has changed a great deal between Bible times and now, so that applying the same rule now would have a result different from its original purpose. This brings us to the next stage:

2. We need to determine the purpose behind any rule that might not be timeless. That is, we need to find the original aim of the rule—the benefit that it produced or harm that it prevented. This is done by looking at the effect of that rule in the various cultures in Bible times. When we have done that, we can decide whether that same rule still applies by asking two questions:

   - If the same rule is used in another society, such as our present one, will it produce the same effect? If the answer is no, then we have to ask:

   - What rule applied in this different society would produce the same effect?

3. The challenging issues which did not exist in ancient times but concern us greatly today still remain—everything from drug abuse to vegetarianism. The chapters concerning these two topics (20 and 29) uncovered some principles that can be applied to any issue that isn't addressed in the Bible. These principles can be summarized as:

   - Avoid anything that may harm us or master us.

- Avoid anything that leads us or others into sinful behavior.

- Avoid anything that brings the gospel into disrepute.

NOW FOR YOUR CONTRIBUTION

Throughout this summary I have referred to examples that "we" have examined. This is because I'm hoping that you now feel able to deal with such issues by yourself and perhaps to question my conclusions in some cases. I laid out my methods and reasoning plainly so that you can check things, and so you might spot factors that I haven't considered properly. You may also interpret the ancient culture in a different way and end up disagreeing with me.

Not everyone can spend years learning ancient languages and decades reading texts from the time of the Bible, but everyone can use a skill that ancient historians need and often neglect: imagination. The key to interpreting the ancient world is partly knowing the material and literary remains, but it is also a matter of imagining the lifestyle and mindset that produced them. We humans have not changed much in the last few thousand years, and your imagination about how people lived and thought in that different society can help you interpret that data as well as anyone else. This means that you may have a different insight into the motivations, inclinations, and hopes of the people who left these artifacts and literature.

This means you may hold a key to understanding an ethical issue that is still causing confusion and perhaps heartache. You now have the tools, and you now know more about the ancient world—and of course there are many other books with details of ancient culture. With these, you should be able to use the Bible to find solutions to moral issues that we are still struggling with.

Index